I Dreamed I Was Normal

*A Music Therapist's Journey
into the Realms of Autism*

Ginger Clarkson

RMT-BC

D1452742

MMB MUSIC, INC.

I DREAMED I WAS NORMAL

Ginger Clarkson, RMT-BC

Cover design: Jill Wade
Typography: A-R Editions, Inc., Madison, Wisconsin
Printer: United Graphics, Inc., Mattoon, Illinois
First printing: October, 1998
Printed in USA
ISBN: 1-58106-007-6

For further information and catalogs, contact:

MMB Music, Inc.
Contemporary Arts Building
3526 Washington Avenue
Saint Louis, MO 63103-1019

Phone: 314 531-9635; 800 543-3771 (USA/Canada)
Fax: 314 531-8384
e-mail: mmbmusic@mmbmusic.com
Web site: http://www.mmbmusic.com

I dedicate this book to Mark B. Ryan,
my soul mate and skillful editor.

Acknowledgments

Many friends and colleagues have helped make this book a reality. I am grateful to my husband Mark B. Ryan and to my mother Virginia Clark Clarkson for their perceptive editorial suggestions. Millie Grenough, Carol Bush, Heidi Ehrenreich, Wink Franklin, Elana Ponet, Nelly Asili, and Don Campbell have my warm appreciation for their thoughtful editorial advice. I thank Tom Winn for deepening my understanding of the work of the Austrian philosopher Rudolph Steiner. Maryann Ott's sensitive eye is reflected in the photographs of artwork that illustrate my text. The psychology department of La Universidad de las Américas in Puebla, Mexico gave this project useful logistical support.

My gratitude goes to the administrators and teachers who have believed in my work as a music therapist. Among them are Amy Lettick, Larry Wood, Linda Grimm, Karen Stevens, Richard Strompf, Dianne Pacyl, and Sarah Murray. Jamie Tardanico, a dedicated speech and language pathologist, helped me make valuable connections between sung and spoken words. Gene Eliasoph, an insightful social worker, kindly invited me to participate in his group therapy sessions for young adults with autism.

I wish to recognize the contributions of Rosemary Crossley, the originator of Facilitated Communication (FC), and of Douglas Biklen, who brought FC from Australia to the United States. I thank Dr. Oliver Sacks for participating in one of my FC sessions and for corresponding with me about the progress of one of the autistic students whose story I tell. I appreciate the generosity of Temple Grandin, who allowed me to guide her in a session of music-evoked imagery, and whose perceptiveness about her own autism gave me important insights. My thanks go to Donna Williams, who wrote me helpful explanations about aspects of her own autistic hypersensitivity. Russell Martin's moving book *Out of Silence,* about the trials of his autistic nephew, inspired me to write about my students who face similar struggles. Without the aid of their mothers, I could not have written these stories about Jerry, Scott and Twyla.

Finally, I am deeply thankful for the guidance and inspiration of my mentors: Vera Moretti, who introduced me to music therapy and inspired me to pursue the field; Helen Bonny, the creator of the Bonny Method of Guided Imagery and Music; and Sierra Stokes and Carol Bush, who trained me in the Bonny Method and who continue to support my work. Blessings to my meditation teacher Jack Kornfield.

Contents

Foreword

This is a book about the revelations of three autistic individuals who came to me for music therapy. When I met Jerry, Scott, and Twyla almost a decade ago, I had no idea how profoundly they would change my assumptions about autism and, for that matter, my entire world view. My initial impression of Jerry was of a tall, muscular African-American man with a bowed head and averted eyes. His inner torment seemed as strong as his corporeal power. Although he could not speak, he communicated both a longing to be recognized and an aversion to physical touch. I felt a magnetic push-pull in his presence. At first sight, Scott affected me less dramatically than Jerry did. He was an active, inquisitive, slightly-built eight-year-old. Constant humming concealed his inability to talk. His blond hair, fair complexion and blue eyes were so attractive I hardly noticed that his face was irregularly shaped and that he had only one ear. He seemed barely to touch the ground as he jumped and danced his way through life. When I met Twyla, she impressed me in her own distinct way. She was a stocky teenager with tousled blond hair and alert blue eyes. Her movements were impatient and impulsive, as if she had no time to waste. She seemed bothered by her hearing aids and removed them whenever possible. Although she seldom spoke intelligibly, Twyla expressed her likes and dislikes clearly by grabbing and throwing objects. These first impressions gave me a mere hint of the intriguing and forceful personalities that I would come to know intimately through years of working together.

In our initial music therapy sessions, as I played the piano and improvised songs, I expected no more than occasional nonverbal responses on simple percussion instruments. But all three students surprised me with the proficiency of their musical improvisations. Later, when the members of this trio learned to type with a technique called Facilitated Communication, I realized that I had vastly underestimated their abilities and knowledge. I felt challenged to adapt a method of music-evoked imagination to their needs. In response to the music, each one typed slowly, letter by letter, descriptions of remarkable images and deep insights. Eventually, they gave striking accounts of their spiritual lives. Independently, Jerry, Scott and Twyla claimed to have chosen to enter this lifetime with autism, so that they could teach normal people to look beyond appearances and to love more fully. Even though I responded to their shared belief system with skepticism, I sensed my own world view expanding.

Twenty-seven years earlier, when I was a music major at Wheaton College in Massachusetts, I happened to see a notice about a music therapy Christmas program to be presented at a nearby institution for residents with disabilities such as mental retardation and autism. Although I had not heard of the field of music therapy, I felt compelled to attend the event. As I drove into the institute's grounds past a formidable row of fortress-like, brick buildings, I had some misgivings. When an unsmiling security guard escorted me from the parking lot to a locked ward, I felt an irrational fear that I might not be able to escape. A tall, lean nurse fumbled through a bunch of keys on a big key ring and admitted me to a large recreation room with pale green walls. Strange sounds, sights and smells assaulted me. Seemingly monstrous beings were rocking and moaning in their chairs beside a piano. One had a head that was half the normal size, while another's head was huge and bloated. Two other faces were missing eyes. I had never before encountered individuals with microcephalia, hydrocephalia, or grotesque physical deformities. I felt overwhelmed and nauseous, and I wanted to flee the scene.

Just as I was about to ask the nurse to unlock the door so that I could leave, an imposing woman entered the room and introduced herself as Vera Moretti, a music therapist. Her intensely blue eyes flashed with fiery determination. Within minutes, Vera's singing and piano accompaniments had transformed the group. Everyone was singing or playing adapted musical instruments or rhythmically moving their limbs. Miraculously, what had seemed a motley crew of malformed creatures became a unified ensemble of dignified performers. Moved to tears, I felt my human connection to the music-makers. Inside each broken body was a whole soul—a musical spirit. I knew at my core that I wanted to become a music therapist.

With Vera's invaluable encouragement and guidance, my conversion experience led to a fulfilling career. Over the course of twenty-five years of work, I have witnessed people of all ages and walks of life transcending anxiety, grief and frustration through music. Within a therapeutic musical milieu, individuals often reveal and identify with a healthy side of themselves. No matter how disabled the participants appear, music seems to soothe their souls and to alleviate their isolation. It is this capacity that music has for breaking down barriers between human beings that motivates me as a music therapist.

By the time I met Jerry, Scott, and Twyla, I had worked as a music therapist for sixteen years following my graduate studies at New York University. I was trained to use an improvisational approach invented by pioneering music therapists Paul Nordoff and Clive Robbins [1983]. Specializing in the field of autism, I was impressed by the power of music to communicate with supposedly unreachable souls. Despite a theoretical orientation that was primarily psychodynamic, I was comfortable using behavioral management techniques, such as positively reinforcing appropriate behaviors and ignoring maladaptive behaviors that were not harmful to people or property. My primary instrument was the piano, but I used guitar, autoharp, resonator bells, drums and various percussion instruments, depending on my students' needs and moods.

First Jerry, and later Scott and Twyla challenged me to move beyond the music therapy techniques and psychiatric labels I had learned in graduate school. They taught me that beneath the awkward and inarticulate surface they present to the world lies sagacity, courage and patience. I feel deeply grateful that they have allowed me to enter their autistic realms and to appreciate a level of musical sensitivity that far surpasses my own. Despite their fears of being ridiculed, these three individuals have encouraged me to write the following chapters about the musical journeys we have traveled together.

I offer these pages to parents and specialists working with people who have autism. Jerry, Scott, and Twyla ask us to enter the world of autism and to see life through their perspective. They ask that we not assume that because they are nonverbal they have nothing to communicate. Each of them has dealt courageously with a malfunctioning body and distorted sensory perceptions. During many years in silence, each has been longing to spread a message of love that our materialistic world sorely needs.

CHAPTER ONE

Jerry

Jerry was not the child his mother had dreamed of having. Nora had been looking forward to having another baby to keep her healthy firstborn son company. Her second pregnancy had been normal until the third month, when she was involved in a minor car accident that jolted her physically and emotionally. During her recovery, she had a premonition that something was not quite right within her womb. She felt worried enough to take a medical leave of absence from her job in a factory for the rest of her pregnancy.

When Nora started having contractions unexpectedly at the beginning of her eighth month, her husband drove her to the hospital as quickly as possible. While helping the short, stocky African-American woman into a wheelchair, the nurse on call was impressed by her patient's quiet dignity and strength. Even though Nora's face was dripping with perspiration and her belly was heaving with contractions, she thanked the nurse for rushing her to the delivery room. There, medical monitors revealed that the heart rate of her fetus was slowing down dangerously. Then, horrifyingly, the screens indicated no heartbeat at all. As she identified with the plight of the child she was carrying, Nora sensed a constriction in her own heart. She could not bear the thought that her child might die before birth. Her obstetrician advised immediate surgery to save the baby's life; and, during the rushed procedures that followed, she heard a voice say, "He's born dead—not enough oxygen." Nora felt inundated by despair and helplessness. What could she have done to prevent such a tragedy?

Then, miraculously, the surgical team was able to revive the preemie. Nora's sobs of grief transformed to tears of gratitude as she tenderly held the three-and-a-half-pound boy. She named him Jarrod. But his birthday—March 27, 1968—was not a day of celebration. He was taken away from his mother and placed in an incubator, his first home for four weeks. As she tried to bond with the infant, Nora was unaware of the likelihood that her child was brain damaged. The medical team did not warn her about developmental problems that might stem from such a traumatic birth experience. By the time she was allowed to take Jarrod home, she felt relieved and hopeful.

Nora gave her baby the nickname Jerry. He was so unresponsive to her hugs and smiles that she relied on his affectionate brother James for reassurance that she was a good mother. The stress of caring for a hyperactive, fussy newborn added tension to her already shaky marriage. By the time Jerry was four years old, his father had left home; and his mother was coping alone with two sons and their baby sister, La Davia. As she filed for divorce two years later, Nora felt grateful for her strong religious faith and the support of her extended family. It was not until Jerry was a teenager that she remarried and delivered her fourth and final child, Lynell.

Nora recalls that although he never developed speech, Jerry responded enthusiastically from infancy to music that he heard at home and at the local Protestant church. Most of the relatives in his extended African-American family were highly musical. Nora inherited perfect pitch from her father and delighted in playing the piano by ear and singing harmonies with her cousins. Jerry's brother, James, worked as a disc jockey; and his sister Lynell studied piano.

According to Nora, Jerry rocked to music as soon as he could sit. Later on, he spent many of his waking hours running around, humming and laughing. If upset, he would wail "eee" in a high-pitched voice. His mother discovered that if she turned on a classical radio program just as he was starting to act distressed, Jerry would crawl onto a rocking chair and rock himself to sleep in rhythm with the music. Whenever she took him to church, from his toddler to teen years, he would sit quietly listening to the hymns and would stay calm during long sermons in order to hear the closing music. At eleven years of age, Jerry amazed the guests at his uncle's wedding reception by jumping up and down and dancing spontaneously for hours to the band music. The skinny youngster seemed oblivious to all but the joy of moving to rhythmic beats. By the age of fourteen, he could play tunes on color-coded piano keys. Even though he was an obvious candidate for music therapy, he had to wait until he was eighteen before he attended a school that employed a music therapist. For nearly twenty years, his musical self was locked inside an isolated and frustrated body.

At age three, Jerry's behavior was so unusual that Nora confessed to a neighbor her concerns that something might be wrong with him. Her neighbor responded that although she had noticed some abnormalities, she had felt hesitant to mention her observations. After this confirmation of her own worries, Nora scheduled her toddler for a thorough neurological evaluation. Jerry was diagnosed as autistic. Nora was devastated to hear from several medical authorities that her child would probably never talk and would have to live in an institution. Partly because Jerry's nonverbal, resistant behavior precluded using standard I.Q. tests, his examiners surmised that he was severely mentally retarded. In spite of the prognosis, Nora stubbornly clung to hope that a cure might be found for her son. Refusing to believe that anyone with such musical responsiveness could be hopelessly retarded, she wondered why tests sensitive enough to measure his innate intelligence had not yet been invented. She enrolled Jerry in a special educational program at the nursery school connected to her church. From four to six years of age, he joined a public school class for mentally retarded children; and, from age six until seventeen, he attended special education classes run by a local agency. Although he learned enough manual sign language to communicate some of his needs, Jerry's behavior grew increasingly unmanageable. Against her better judgment, Nora permitted a school doctor to prescribe first Mellaril and then Benadril to sedate her adolescent son. She was not surprised when neither drug had significant effects.

Throughout his educational career, numerous psychologists and psychiatrists put Jerry through a variety of tests, including the Peabody Picture Vocabulary Test, the Goodenough-Harris Draw-a-Man Test, and the Vineland Test of Social Maturity. The results were wildly contradictory. His I.Q. scores ranged from thirty-nine to seventy-nine; his mental age was estimated to be from two to eight years, and his diagnoses varied from profound to mild levels of mental retardation. All of his examiners found Jerry's volatile and compulsive behaviors to be a deterrent during testing. Although she could not convince the specialists, Nora sensed intuitively that hidden behind her son's repellent conduct was an intelligent human being.

By age thirteen, with his frequent temper tantrums, Jerry had virtually destroyed the family apartment. He was now taller than his grayhaired mother, and she could no longer control him physically. Reluctantly, she allowed a concerned social worker to place him in a residential institution for mentally retarded students. The experiment lasted nine months. It was a disaster. Jerry had trouble sleeping in the crowded ward that was lined with beds. The harried staff members were too overworked to give their unruly teenage charges individual attention, aside from disciplining them. Jerry's behavior worsened. By the time he was transferred to another residence, he had become habitually withdrawn and frequently aggressive to anyone who interfered with his numerous compulsive behaviors. Following an elaborate set of rituals, he took over an hour to get dressed each morning. Before tying his shoes, Jerry would carefully cross and uncross the laces as many as a hundred times. It was no wonder that his caretakers lost patience while they prodded him to complete the most basic chores.

Appalled by her son's condition, Nora consulted a new doctor who attempted to control Jerry's compulsions with a series of medications. After subsequent trials with Haldol, Thorazine and Prolixin, the doctor admitted that none of the drugs was producing more than negative side effects. Jerry suffered from dry mouth, drowsiness and dizzy spells, and his vision seemed to be deteriorating. Because he could not speak about his symptoms, his medications needed more careful monitoring than was possible in his group residence. The doctor decided to discontinue all medications, but he promised to inform Nora if research on newly invented designer drugs warranted more experiments with Jerry.

Nora felt increasingly discouraged about her son's prognosis. Only an unshakable religious faith and the loving support of her second husband kept her battling on Jerry's behalf. She now had a partner who was a hard-working, responsible man. He made an effort to befriend the three children from her first marriage. Even though he had never before met anyone with autism, he treated Jerry respectfully and understood how deeply his wife loved the withdrawn and restless teenager. But Nora was still on her own when it came to handling the crises that erupted regularly in her son's life.

When he was barely seventeen, Jerry was expelled from his residential school for repeated incidents of aggression and for bolting out of the classroom. Only after his mother sued their hometown to provide him with a mandated day program were arrangements made for private tutoring. After more than a year of largely unproductive work, Jerry seemed at a dead end. In desperation, Nora managed to have him admitted to a group home and a private special education program, both of which were better suited to his needs. At last, he was in settings where both his teachers and residential staff could collaborate in reinforcing his use of manual sign language, thus teaching him some clerical and maintenance work skills and employing behavioral management techniques to redirect his violent outbursts.

It was at this time that Jerry showed a real affinity for music and even imitated some basic ballroom dancing steps. When I was hired as the school's music therapist in 1988, Jerry was at the top of a list of candidates for me to assess. But before I met him, Amy, the principal, prepared me to expect violent episodes. Because she herself was the mother of a grown son with autism, she spoke assuredly from years of experience. Her dark eyes reflected both determination and fatigue. Amy had founded the school after failing in a nationwide search for a suitable educational program for her child. I respected her reputation as an authority in the field of autism.

Amy described how Jerry had been having daily temper tantrums, each lasting an hour or more. Typically, he would moan and howl in frustration, hitting his ears with his fists or pounding his head against walls until he drew blood. His latest outbursts stemmed from an inability to bring himself to climax while masturbating, and from staff who attempted to escort him to an empty room for more privacy. Like many nonverbal people with disabilities, Jerry had received no sexual education and did not know how to release his pent-up libidinous energy in socially acceptable ways. During tantrums, he would lash out to hit or kick anyone who intervened, and he would often damage property. Because he had repeatedly smashed window panes, light fixtures, and appliances in his bedroom, the window had been covered with plywood, and all furniture had been removed except for his bed. Since Jerry was then six feet tall and very powerful, at least three trained staff were required in order to restrain his violent behavior. Witnesses of his explosive episodes reported that Jerry had occasionally blurted out "No!" and "Sit down!" at the height of a crisis, and "Yes!" and "Get up!" when restrained. This "tantrum talk" was his only sign of intelligible speech.

Despite her serious warnings about his behavior, Amy referred to Jerry so compassionately that I intuitively shared her respect for his daily struggles to make sense out of the world around him. She reported that although he destroyed any glasses with prescription lenses designed to correct his severe myopia, he would fashion his own spectacles and masks spontaneously from cardboard and cellophane. He had discovered that he could improve his vision by peeking through tiny peepholes in the center of his hand-crafted glasses. Such ingenuity indicated that Jerry had an intelligent mind. I began to feel excited about meeting this troubled young man who possessed obvious musical and artistic abilities.

Because of their distortions in sensory processing, most people with autism appreciate sameness in their environment and consistency in their daily routines. I decided to employ a Nordoff-Robbins music therapy technique of clearly structuring sessions by beginning with a greeting song and ending with a farewell song. Between these two songs I planned to encourage Jerry to imitate rhythmic patterns on drums, play accompaniments on a selection of melodic instruments, and dance to recorded music. Since I was determined to treat him as much as possible as a responsible adult, my goal was to enhance his self-esteem and autonomy by developing his musical skills. I aimed to expose Jerry to a variety of songs and instruments, because I hoped that he would be tempted to communicate his preferences. But, despite all my planning, I had no idea how he would receive my overtures.

On a gray March day, Jerry's teacher ushered him into my music room for his first music therapy session. As I observed his outer appearance—the bruised and averted face, the lowered eyes, and the slouched posture—I sensed a profound inner depression. He passively accepted my invitation to sit down by the piano, and he watched warily as I sang a greeting song with a simple accompaniment on two resonator bells. Jerry allowed me to give him the bell mallet, which he grasped in his dominant left hand. He would not let me touch his rigid wrist to help him rebound the mallet, and interrupted his playing periodically to lick his hands in a ritualistic fashion. He appeared to be more relaxed when he used two drumsticks to beat a standing drum. After only one run-through, Jerry could beat in perfect rhythm to an improvised piece that required him to switch from one to two hands on cue. Not only was he able to follow my changes in tempo and dynamics on the piano, but he also anticipated phrase endings and cadences in the music. I noticed that his motor development was delayed; he tended to use simultaneous bilateral arm movements and to avoid crossing his body's midline. Surprisingly, for a man of his strength, his beating was quite timid and soft. When I introduced "Fun for Four Drums," a drumming game by Nordoff and Robins, Jerry initially beat an accompaniment with only one hand. Despite his being able to copy a demonstration of alternating drumsticks, his arms moved slowly and awkwardly in this new motor pattern; and he had trouble keeping up with the tempo of the piano. Since he seemed to like the challenge of practicing a new musical skill, I slowed the piano part to match his tempo. I was careful to stop the activity before he became discouraged.

I then used manual sign language to prepare Jerry for a period of dancing to a recording of "La Bamba," which his teacher had told me was one of his favorite songs. At this beginning stage of our moving together, he stood facing me, watching carefully from a distance of several yards. Whatever gesture or step I initiated, he copied, but he made no effort to add any motions of his own. Recognizing that his most fluid movements were above the waist, I began by moving only the upper body, and then just the lower body, slowly stepping to the back, front and sides. As Jerry grew more confident about maintaining his balance, I experimented with combining upper and lower body movements as well as stretching up on tiptoes, crouching down low, circling around, and twisting the torso. I felt encouraged by his efforts to imitate me. Although his legs and feet still lagged behind his arms, Jerry's body movements began to look more coordinated.

Once he had expanded his repertoire by copying me in this non-threatening way, Jerry was amenable to playing two resonator bells to accompany a farewell song. During his first attempt, he double-beat each bell, but after he watched a second demonstration, he played the bells correctly, once each in sequence. He seemed satisfied with his achievement and even risked a glance at my face before he left the room. We had made a musical connection.

In the weeks that followed, Jerry gradually grew accustomed to beginning each session with a greeting song and closing with a farewell song, but any change in routine disturbed him. One day, to make room for dancing, I folded a new collapsible chair that had just been installed in the music room. In response to this break with the usual routine, Jerry threw himself on the floor and started moaning and hitting himself on his ears. I felt frightened and helpless to prevent his self-abuse. His tantrum accelerated when I called for extra staff to help, and two hours passed before he calmed down. In the aftermath of that session, I was very careful to prepare Jerry for any changes. To help him feel oriented in time, his classroom teacher instituted a daily picture schedule, using photographs of different activities in the sequence in which he would be experiencing them. Each day he had music therapy they inserted a picture of me seated at the piano.

After six months of sessions, Jerry entered a second phase of social interaction and musical progress. He started making frequent eye contact and smiling whenever he successfully completed a rhythmic task. He spontaneously used sign language to communicate "hello," "good-bye," "dance," "more," and the numbers "one" through "ten." In addition, he readily imitated manual signs for the colors identifying specific resonator bells. Once I had taught him to shake his left wrist to loosen it up, he could rebound a mallet to produce a clear, ringing tone. I was impressed by his superb auditory memory for short melodic patterns that he had learned in previous sessions. While he was dancing, Jerry was increasingly comfortable with being touched. If I approached him

slowly, offering my hands, he would hold hands with me for brief periods of time, twirl me around, walk next to me, and sway directly opposite me. His long, tapered fingers grasped mine so gently that I almost
forgot how destructive his large hands could be. Between dance numbers, Jerry often manually signed "more" to indicate that he wanted to
continue dancing. No longer was he merely copying my movements. If
I waited patiently, he would initiate a few of his own.

In six months of practice, Jerry's drumming had improved as much
as his dancing. He had learned to alternate drumsticks smoothly and
rapidly, and he could differentiate among four different call-and-
response rhythmic patterns. He mastered the configurations, one by
one, by listening and watching carefully as I modeled them on the
drum. After he had practiced each rhythmic grouping several times, I
started mixing cues for two distinct patterns. Jerry would pay close
attention and smile each time he figured out which one was required.
Once he had mastered discriminating between two patterns, it was a
relatively easy task to add a third, and later a fourth. I was touched by
his eagerness to learn new skills. He acknowledged each achievement
with a glint of excitement in his dark eyes. When I corrected his infre-
quent errors, he was receptive and patiently revised the rhythm. He still
needed encouragement, however, to play with force and assertiveness.

After a year of music therapy sessions that were focused on drumming and dancing, Jerry moved into a third phase marked by his growing interest in melodic instruments. Playing a set of resonator bells
arranged like a piano keyboard, he was able to pick out the sequence of
tones to several familiar melodies. He wrinkled his brow in concentration and hunched over the bells. At first he played slowly and cau-
tiously, and he found it difficult to reverse direction on the bells. But
after I modeled keeping the mallet close to the surface of the bells to
ensure accuracy during fast tempos, Jerry mastered a rapid accompaniment to a song in ABA form. He learned to reverse direction in the
middle of playing the "A" theme, to rest patiently while I played the
"B" theme on the piano, and to play on cue as soon as the "A" theme
recurred. As we completed our first melodic duet, I sensed that Jerry
shared my pride in his accomplishment. He became so absorbed in
practicing this bell accompaniment that on one occasion he persevered
while a workman was hammering nails in the hallway and a student
was screaming in the next room.

It was during Jerry's second year of music therapy that he began to
follow color-coded musical notation. I introduced him to the concept

of notation by reviewing a bell accompaniment to a song he knew well. He was able to sign manually the different colors on the dots marking each of the five bells he had just played. I then showed him a file card on which similarly colored dots were arranged in a sequence from left to right. As Jerry watched with obvious interest, I pointed to the dot on the first bell and then to the dot farthest left on the card, making sure that he understood that they matched. After pointing out the correlation between all the colored markers on the bells and those on the card, I asked Jerry to do the same. Once he successfully completed the task, I directed him to play the bells as I pointed to corresponding dots on the file card. His rapt attention and grins indicated his excitement about comprehending this new approach to playing music. Once he understood the concept of notation, Jerry was able to perform increasingly difficult bell accompaniments, including ones that required distinguishing between two melodic lines. Because of his visual orientation, notation facilitated his memorization of a number of melodies. I felt excited by his newfound ability to express the musicality that he embodied.

In our third year together, Jerry's fourth phase of music therapy was characterized by a marked improvement in self-esteem and by active interaction with me. To accommodate his expanded attention span, I extended his sessions from a half-hour to fifty minutes. By this time, not only was he receptive when rhythmic or melodic errors were pointed out to him, but he also learned quickly from his mistakes, because he seldom repeated one. Jerry rarely engaged in the compulsive mannerisms that formerly interrupted his performance, and he was responsible about putting away musical instruments at the end of the sessions. His drumming skills had improved to such a degree that he could accompany a waltz played on the piano. Through every measure of this lengthy piece, he steadily beat a drum once and a standing cymbal twice. Jerry's progress in following musical notation enabled him to tackle a complex bell accompaniment to a piano arrangement of J.S. Bach's "Jesu, Joy of Man's Desiring." Without any lyrics to guide him, he anticipated each recurrence of the opening melodic line, with which he played contrapuntal harmony on six resonator bells. I celebrated his blossoming as a musician.

During dance routines, Jerry took my place operating the portable stereo. He was relaxed enough to initiate gestures and steps and to hold hands with me throughout entire songs. Not only would he twirl me in and out, but he also allowed me to do the same to him. While dancing,

Jerry's posture straightened, his eye contact was steady, and his expression was smiling. The movements of his feet were increasingly synchronized with the motions of his upper body, so that his dancing looked graceful.

Jerry no longer needed prompting to sign manually "good-bye, Ginger" at the end of sessions. One day an observer took Polaroid pictures while Jerry and I were dancing together and playing the familiar farewell song. When he looked at the photographs, Jerry pointed to himself and to me and smiled. In response to my sign language, "We are friends," he signed a silent but emphatic "yes."

On that afternoon in 1992, I did not anticipate how central this friendship would become to my own spiritual growth.

CHAPTER TWO

Scott

Janice admits that when she discovered that she was pregnant for the fifth time, she was unpleasantly surprised. She was busy raising three active girls, aged nine, eight and six, and their four-year-old brother. At age thirty-five, she had not planned to have another child, especially since she and her husband Joe were having marital problems. But in coming to terms with the situation, the slim, energetic mother recalled that before she married she had proclaimed that she would have five children. She recognized that she was flourishing in her maternal role, as she delighted in her children's appreciation of small details around them. As a practicing Catholic, she did not even consider having an abortion. When she was five months pregnant, however, she started having premature contractions. After diagnosing an incompetent cervix, her obstetrician ordered bed rest for the remainder of the pregnancy. Janice's water broke prematurely at thirty-five weeks.

When Scott was born on January 27, 1982, his mother noticed right away that he had no left ear. His tiny face appeared unbalanced because of a facial palsy; both eyes moved irregularly with the left one unable to blink; and his spine was twisted with scoliosis, due to a missing rib on one side of his body and an extra rib on the other side. Almost immediately, the baby was taken away for a week of extensive testing at a nearby children's hospital. Janice felt more distressed by her son's impersonal initiation to life than by his slight deformities. She wondered how the invasive medical examinations would affect him. An initial hearing test revealed that his right ear had normal acuity, and that he did not have any of the kidney problems that are often associated with a missing ear.

The pediatrician's official term for Scott's ear, eye and spinal abnormalities was "Goldenhar's syndrome." It is often associated with mental retardation. At the time of Scott's birth, this syndrome was so rare that few doctors had ever seen a case. A decade later, however, Janice read that after the Desert Storm troops were exposed to chemical weapons in the Gulf War, the incidence increased to one in every 65,000 births. When a genetic counselor asked Janice if she had noticed anything unusual about her pregnancy, she remembered that in her second month, she had used chemicals to spray some fruit trees in back of her house. She will never know if that chemical exposure contributed to Scott's condition, but her attitude was constructive: "You can't change the past. All you can do is make the future better."

After raising four children, Janice was an experienced mother. Although her youthful face had few wrinkles, her short-cropped light brown hair was beginning to show flecks of gray. She was not phased by her youngest child's appearance. She decided to nurse Scott and to treat him just the way she had his older brothers and sisters. When he was seven months old, however, he restlessly turned his head to observe details in his environment and stopped nursing on his own. Several months later, as he started to crawl, he would bang his head on the stove each time he entered the kitchen and then follow the lines imprinted on the linoleum floor.

Having no knowledge of autism at this point, Janice attributed many of her son's unusual behaviors to his visual impairment—a horizontal nystagmus. During an early eye examination, an optometrist told her that because of the rapid side to side movements of his eyes, Scott could not be expected to see beyond ten feet, and that he would be considered legally blind. Although he could see well enough at close range to learn to read, he would have trouble riding a bicycle because of his limited far vision. Janice questioned why her little boy was so fascinated by spinning objects, why he liked to rock back and forth or to be rocked, and why riding in cars or on swings or merry-go-rounds gave him special pleasure. The optometrist explained that many children with nystagmus find it restful to watch and engage in whirling motions.

Janice was accustomed to coping with a range of developmental milestones. While her daughter Melanie had surprised everyone by walking early at nine months, her son Michael had not walked until he was fourteen months old. But even though she knew that boys tend to develop later than girls, Janice was concerned when Scott reached eighteen months without walking independently. Refusing to accept her outstretched hand, he would tolerate physical touch only when he initiated it himself. Although he would grab her hand or pant leg for support and toddle along beside her, he would sit down as soon as she moved away. To Janice, it was as if he were making the silent statement: "I can't walk on my own." Scott also resisted toilet training, and even as a teenager, he would defecate in his pants when he was upset. Janice worried that the toddler would put any object he encountered into his mouth. She would catch him chewing on cardboard or wood, and she had to be vigilant that he did not swallow dangerous items. She noticed that at the age of one, Scott had spoken a few individual words such as "Mama" and "Papa," but that his speech did not develop beyond that point. On the contrary, it deteriorated, and he stopped articulating any consonants.

When he was eighteen months old, Janice enrolled her little tow-headed boy in an early intervention program sponsored by the Connecticut State Department of Mental Retardation. Scott's teachers used Total Communication, a technique that integrates spoken and signed language. By the age of two, he had learned ten manual signs, but he never added to his repertoire and seemed uninterested in this form of communication. At three and a half years old, Scott was diagnosed as being multiply handicapped with autistic tendencies. After reading every book she could find about autism, Janice negotiated with the local school board for her son to transfer to a structured special education program in a small class of five children. But just as Scott was demonstrating that he could understand simple directions receptively, the program was dissolved. The children were dispersed to different public schools in larger special education classes that contained students with severe behavioral disorders.

By this time, Scott's vocalizations consisted mostly of vowels sounds such as "ah," "ou," "oh," or "ee." With coaching, he would attempt to imitate two-syllable words: "oo-ee" signified "cookie." Sometimes he ground his teeth or made soft clicking sounds with his tongue. Even when he switched abruptly to a louder volume, these noises did not seem to have any communicative intent. Scott often whistled and made tonal approximations of short phrases, duplicating perfectly the intonation and rhythmic stress of questions such as "How are you?" But aside from his family and a few educators who knew him well, nobody could decipher the songlike strings of vowel sounds that the expressive child was uttering.

Regardless of his communication problems, his siblings treated Scott affectionately and included him in their practical jokes and games. One way that Janice handled arguments among her five children was to institute puppet shows in which the puppets could squabble to their heart's content. Scott was especially drawn to a lion puppet, and he would enact the little lion chasing himself. One Christmas his mother gave him a stuffed mouse that she named "Chris Mouse." Every night as Scott was settling into bed, Janice would have the mouse kiss him good night on his nose or neck. The child's response was to bounce the mouse down into his arms for an affectionate hug. These hugging rehearsals inspired Scott on rare occasions to surprise and delight his mother or one of his siblings by giving them a brief spontaneous hug. It took him longer to feel comfortable exchanging back scratches with members of his family. After tiring of filling her older children's numerous requests for individual back rubs, Janice invented a circular "scratching train" so that everyone in the family could give and receive a back scratch simultaneously. At first Scott shied away from this physical contact, but gradually he was tempted to join the train. Through such gentle games, he learned to accept the physical touch that had been so aversive.

Scott worked hard to overcome fears stemming from hypersensitivity to noise. When he was small, he hated low-pitched vibrating sounds made by blow driers and other appliances. His mother recalls that during his initial trip to a dentist, Scott froze and broke out into a cold sweat as soon as he heard the sound of the drill. The first time the family's barber, Gary, used an electric buzz cutter on him, he screamed, cried, and stiffened his whole body in resistance. But Scott seemed to realize that if he were going to interact freely in the world around him, he would have to build up a tolerance for noise. With Gary's cooperation and Janice's patient encouragement, he gradually learned to tolerate the sound of the buzzer at a distance for short periods of time. Then Gary offered the buzzer for the boy to touch briefly. The next time he came for a haircut, Scott tolerated the buzzer first on his hand and then on his neck. Although his grimaces made it obvious that the tickling sensation bothered him, he used sign language to indicate that "yes," the barber should continue. The day that he withstood his first buzz-cut, Scott grinned with pride. He could see in the barber's mirror that his hairstyle resembled that of his revered older brother Michael.

The first time he experienced an electric hand drier in a public bathroom, Scott bolted out of the room. But the next time he heard one, he made himself stay in the room, albeit he was as far away as possible from the offending noise. One of his teachers remembers the day that he ran up to a hand drier, pushed the button, and ran laughing to the other side of the room. He had created a game that he could use in other settings to desensitize himself to aversive sounds. One of Scott's variations on this theme was pushing the forbidden button on the fire alarm in his home. Until his mother discouraged this practice, he would set off a loud siren and run away convulsed with laughter.

Janice respected how hard her son worked to surmount his fears. She assumed that he had at least normal intelligence. Her older children absorbed her positive attitude and never teased Scott about being autistic or retarded. Upon the advice of a wise pediatrician, Janice did not coddle him, and she was not afraid to tell him when his behavior made her angry. If he screamed in the middle of a crowded supermarket, for example, she would warn him that unless he stopped, he would have to leave. Likewise, his siblings did not hesitate to tell him to stop if he bothered them or used their possessions without permission. Although their criticism upset him, Scott sensed that he was treated fairly as a member of the family team. He complied when Janice asked him to do his share of household chores, such as dusting and vacuuming. He liked being rewarded for good behavior with hugs, verbal praise, or snacks such as raisins and apples. Because the entire family had high expectations for his behavior, he learned a clear sense of right and wrong.

Among Scott's strengths was a mechanical adeptness. Throughout his childhood, he enjoyed taking apart and putting together toys and appliances. One of his favorite toys was called "Steel Tech," an assortment of nuts, bolts, screws, rods, and wheels that he spent hours assembling in various combinations. He may have inherited some of this skill from his father's brother, who is a genius at repairing motorcycles and machines. Janice wisely recruited her son to fix broken door hinges and to do other home repairs. He looked gratified whenever he was applying his mechanical abilities constructively.

But nothing thrilled Scott more than opportunities to show off his musical talents. He was blessed to grow up in a highly musical family who appreciated his ability and creativity in that realm. Both sisters took weekly piano lessons in the home. Janice's brother is a professional singer and guitarist, and her mother and maternal grandmother both played piano since early childhood. One of Janice's uncles was blind but could play the piano eloquently. Whenever these extended family members visited, they would play music and sing with Scott. When he was about two years old, the mobile toddler amazed his mother by crawling onto the piano bench and picking out the tune to "Mary Had a Little Lamb" with barely a glitch. Shortly afterwards, he astounded his classroom teacher with his musical ingenuity. While she was trying to figure out why he was screaming angrily, Scott pointed to a classmate who had just stolen his toy truck and sang the tune to a 'truck song' that she had taught the children hours earlier.

Janice noticed early on that her son had perfect pitch and that he could hum flawlessly the tunes to Christmas carols and other songs. Scott would sing in the same key as the melody was played when he first heard it and stay true to pitch throughout his rendition. As a young boy, he would sing himself to sleep, humming one of about fifty tunes that he had memorized. During waking hours, it was seldom that the family stereo was not playing. After dinner, the whole family would dance to Barry Manilow recordings in the living room. Although he preferred dancing solo, Scott could be coaxed to do slow partner danc-ing with his mother or his sister Cindy, who taught him to twirl her around. To calm the children down after dancing, Janice established a routine of playing soothing recordings before bedtime.

In spite of his numerous skills and strengths, Scott's odd behaviors and communicative difficulties became so worrisome by the time he was six and a half years old that Janice scheduled him for a psychiatric evaluation. She told the examining physician that she had never seen her son smile socially or make eye contact with anyone. Although he would seek affection by putting his arm around his parents, or by indi-cating through gestures that he wanted them to scratch his back, he would sometimes push away his mother when she approached him. Not only had he never participated in baby games such as "Peekaboo" or "Pattycake," but also he did not play at all with classmates at school.

At the time of the evaluation, his teacher had just reported an odd incident in the classroom. All her students except for Scott were at the window watching a dog run around on the playground. The youngsters started hollering, "here, doggie," to attract the dog's attention. Almost unnoticed, Scott quietly approached the window and touched his nose to the glass. At that instant, the dog spun around and trotted straight over to place its nose against the window pane directly opposite Scott's face. His teacher and classmates were stunned by this apparent display of nonverbal communication.

Because he showed no fear of ordinary dangers such as traffic or heights, Scott required constant supervision. On several occasions, he ran away from home and had to be traced. During one search outside, Janice looked up and saw her small blond son sitting calmly atop the roof of the garage. He had shinnied up the TV antenna pole, but he needed a rescue party to help him descend. Shortly after the family moved to a new home in a neighborhood not far from their former house, Scott disappeared. In the midst of Janice's panic-stricken phone calls, a woman arrived, escorting the unrepentant runaway. The lady explained that she had discovered the six-year-old boy in her pantry eating cookies. Although he did not speak, his blue eyes communicated that he felt right at home in her house and was in no rush to leave. Upon hearing the address of his destination, Janice realized that her helpful neighbor owned the house that used to belong to Scott's great-aunt and great-uncle. He had last visited there three years earlier, shortly before the death of his great-uncle. Nobody could explain the youngster's homing instinct, because he had never before walked the circuitous route from one house to the other.

More than his running away, Janice was concerned about Scott's compulsive rituals. She noticed that he seemed to have a cyclical pattern of increased energy that peaked each wintertime. Each time they left the house, she had to wait while Scott jumped, twirled around, and then fiddled with the Velcro straps on his sneakers. Before he felt settled in a room, he had to make sure that all drawers and doors were shut. During his inexplicable attempts to keep all the windows uncovered, he destroyed curtains, window shades, and venetian blinds. While he busied himself at home, Scott never played with toys in a conventional way; but, instead, he arranged pieces of furniture in particular patterns around the house. Once he even tried to place one of his sisters in a long line of chairs and tables. He was so obsessed with some of his T-shirts that he would trash rooms until he found them. Once, when his parents locked his room to prevent him from fetching a favorite T-shirt, Scott hollered, kicked, and threw objects for nearly an hour.

The examining physician diagnosed the youngster as having an autistic disorder after listening to Janice's long list of concerns and unsuccessfully trying to engage Scott in various interactive games. Noting that both parents and their four normal children were under significant stress trying to keep up with such a hyperactive boy, the doctor recommended that Scott be placed in a residential school that would allow him to come home for weekend visits. Sadly acknowledging that his departure would benefit the whole family, Janice began the long application process for her hometown school system to provide funding for a reputable residential program an hour away.

On her application form, Janice described a normal day in the family's routine. As soon as Scott woke up, anywhere between 5:30 and 7:00 a.m., his mother would get up to have him shower with her, so she could make sure that he cleaned his entire body. After she gave him a choice of two shirts to wear, Scott would dress himself. To indicate his choices for breakfast, he would point to a bagel or oatmeal and push away less desired food. Once Janice left for her job as an administrative coordinator of economic development in the local town hall, her son Michael would supervise Scott playing on a swing set until their school bus arrived at 8:10. Because she had special permission to leave work early enough to be home to greet Scott's bus at 3:00, Janice worked on Saturdays to make up the lost time. On weekday afternoons, she would try to take her slim, vivacious child for a walk or a swim to help him expend energy in a safe and fun way. When the older children returned from competing on various sports teams, they would decide whose turn it was to change their little brother's soiled clothing. Then Janice would cook supper while Scott helped Michael set the table. By the time the girls had helped wash the dishes, and all the children had had a brief recreation period before they did their homework, Scott needed help to wash up, brush his teeth and change into his pajamas. His mother and siblings had a rotating schedule to assist him with his bed-time routine. If all went smoothly, Scott would be in bed with lights out by 8:30 p.m. Janice was grateful that her effervescent son would sleep for nine or ten hours each night.

His family experienced a mixture of sadness and relief as the eight-year-old boy left home for boarding school in June of 1990. Coinci-dentally, he was assigned to a classroom near the music room, and I nearly bumped into the shy, fair-haired newcomer as I was escorting Jerry to a music therapy session. Scott seemed wary of me and my tall companion, more than ten years his senior. It took several months for the new boy to adjust to new routines in classes, at meals, and at bed-time. His classroom teacher Debbie treated him with an effective blend of respectful firmness and kindness. She made sure that he had daily periods of strenuous exercise to help him release energy and that he made a trip to the bathroom every two hours to prevent accidents. In order to discourage his tendency to disassemble and break objects in class, she arranged a "fix-it" box of items that he was allowed to take apart. Although he rarely interacted spontaneously with his classmates, Scott did learn to wait his turn and to help out in group projects. Deb-bie taught him to look both ways before he crossed streets and to notice stop lights and traffic signs. On field trips to McDonald's and Stop and Shop, he practiced using the coins he had learned to identify. Slowly, he learned to curb his loud vocalizing and to indicate "no" with sign language rather than with screams.

The main focus of Scott's schooling was to improve his ability to communicate his needs and desires. His receptive comprehension of language was excellent, and his teachers soon realized that whenever he did not respond to their questions or directions, he was conveying a nonverbal form of protest. To help him express himself more precisely, his speech-language therapist gave him a picture-word communication book composed of Mayer-Johnson drawings, each a square inch in size, illustrating actions, emotions, objects, and locations. She added photos of key people in Scott's life. An identifying word was printed beneath each picture, and the vocabulary was organized and color-coded according to categories. It did not take Scott long to learn that if he needed to go to the bathroom or if he wanted a snack, he could approach his teachers with the book and point to the picture that matched his desire. Scott's keen interest in reading motivated him to train his own nystagmic eye muscles to slow down and even stop for short periods of time.

In his residential home, he was trained to use an Epson laptop computer with a MemKey overlay. The device had a digital voice that would vocalize words he typed or pictures he pushed. On home visits, Janice instituted a simple but clever communicative system to help her son express choices. If she were going to take him to a restaurant, for instance, she would hold his nondominant right hand, touch the middle finger, and label it "McDonald's." Once he understood that his ring finger represented "Friendly's" and his pointer stood for "Burger King," Scott would point to the finger that matched his preference. Before taking him out for lunch, his mother would check to make sure that he chose the same option twice. His grin and his squeals of pleasure as she drove him to the restaurant of his choice left no doubt that this decision-making procedure was valid.

From the moment that I met Scott—he was then eight years old—it was obvious that music therapy was a prime way to motivate him to communicate. Because of his family's history of music-making, he was scheduled to join his four classmates for regular group music therapy sessions shortly after he entered the school. Scott's musical connection with me was instantaneous. When he arrived for his first session, his face lit up as soon as he saw my piano. As I began to sing "Hello," he glanced over at me and hummed a few tones in the same key as the song. During his turn to choose from an assortment of simple percussion instruments, he examined several from Latin America in minute detail. He was fascinated by the rattling sound he could make by rubbing the metal beads on the cabasa and the scratching noise created by running a metal comb over the serrated surface of the guiro. He was equally captivated by the watery sound of tiny pebbles passing from one end of the rainstick to the other each time he turned it. If I had not intervened to help him make a selection, Scott might have spent the entire morning exploring the possibilities of every instrument in the room. He finally settled on a bright orange set of jingle bells. After only one demonstration, he recalled when to start and stop playing in the song "Jingle Bells." Because of his extraordinary sensitive sense of rhythm, he picked up precisely how fast to shake the bells. He effort-lessly assumed the role of leader in his music therapy group, and demonstrated instrumental parts for his classmates.

In the months that followed, Scott experimented enthusiastically on a wide range of musical instruments and memorized a specific accom-paniment on each one. He liked to move his body rhythmically to music, either alone or with a partner. Jumping was one of his favorite pastimes; he especially enjoyed following the instructions of a song called "Jump in and Out." While I sang, he would coordinate his actions with my lyrics by leaping in and out of a hula hoop lying on the floor. After performing the sequence twice, he would circumvent the hoop and then sit down, just as the song ended. With a little prac-tice, he learned to rock gracefully back and forth and to swing his arms from side to side in coordination with a partner's movements. Once he mastered a routine, however, Scott did not like to change its pattern. One day, when I substituted the piano for the guitar that I usually used to play the farewell song, he fetched the guitar case, took out the instrument and started strumming the strings. His message could not have been clearer.

Shortly thereafter, I rescheduled Scott for more advanced music therapy sessions with another nonverbal autistic student who was named Gabe. Initially, each boy resisted the change by acting as if the other did not exist. While I was focusing on Gabe playing an instru-ment of his choice, Scott would be vocalizing to himself, staring at the ceiling, or rocking back and forth in his chair. Gabe was equally unin-terested in his classmate's musical exchanges with me. But gradually, as the youngsters realized that a familiar structure remained in between the well-known greeting and farewell songs, Scott and Gabe began to pay attention to one another. My role was to tempt them to interact socially, to encourage them to pass instruments back and forth, and to orchestrate short instrumental duets. One day I was delighted to wit-ness Gabe pointing to a pattern of stars on his shirt as he listened to Scott figuring out the melody to "Twinkle, Twinkle Little Star" on a set of resonator bells. Although Gabe avoided physical contact with me, Scott became accustomed to sitting in my lap as I guided his left forefinger to play the melody of the farewell waltz on my keyboard. Before he left the music room, he often showed off his ability to play "Mary Had a Little Lamb" by memory on the black keys. Scott appeared genuinely pleased by my praise and congratulatory hugs for his performances. After several years of celebrating his slow but steady progress in social contact via music, I heard the news of major upheaval in his family.

By the time Scott was twelve, Janice had asked Joe for an amicable divorce and moved into her own apartment. For many years, she had felt like a single mother because her husband had been so busy with his job as a letter carrier during weekdays. Every other weekend he had been away from home, serving as a sergeant in the Air Force Reserves. Joe admitted to being somewhat autistic in his own routines, because he liked meals served in specific ways at particular times. Since he was a withdrawn man, he seldom hugged or initiated physical contact with his children. But despite his aloofness, it was clear that he loved his family. Although he did not know how to handle his youngest son, Joe did his best to relate to Scott.

All five children went through a period of emotional turmoil related to their parents' separation. Even though he was visiting from school only on alternate weekends, Scott had an especially hard time dealing with two homes. He missed the furniture that his mother moved out of the family's house and kept pointing to where a familiar brown chair had been in the living room. When he first visited his mother's new apartment, he did not want to stay until he spotted the brown chair. He was accustomed to sharing the overstuffed recliner with his mother on evenings when they watched television together, and when she would scratch his back. Scott ran over to operate the lever on his side of the chair. Having established his territorial rights, he smiled and gave his nonverbal blessing to his second home.

In the aftermath of his parents' divorce, however, Scott's behavior regressed temporarily at school. During a psychological evaluation at age thirteen, he was assessed as having the motor skills of a four-year-old, the social skills of a one-and-a-half-year-old toddler, the personal living skills of a child less than half his age, and the community living skills of a three-and-a half-year-old. Because he was slightly built and small for his age, he appeared much younger than his classmates. According to the *Inventory for Client and Agency Planning*, Scott's level of "broad independence" had not developed beyond that of a four-year-old. After evaluating him with the Leiter Test, a nonverbal measure of cognitive skills, the psychologist concluded that Scott had a mental age of about four years old and that his performance was moderately to severely retarded. His family and teachers would have found this assessment dismaying had he not been showing remarkable progress at the very same time in music therapy and in speech/language therapy.

I had no premonition that Scott's progress would far surpass my most hopeful dreams about his future.

CHAPTER THREE

Twyla

Mary recalls that the birth of her only child, Twyla, felt precious, particularly since the pregnancy followed many months of unsuccessful efforts to conceive a child. In the aftermath of several artificial insemination attempts at a fertility clinic, she and her husband Jack were about to give up their dream of having a baby. After completing her master's degree in education, Mary reluctantly faced the possibility that teaching second graders in a public school would be the closest she would come to mothering. Although she tried not to let her disappointment interfere with her work, her principal noticed that the blond, small-boned teacher was looking fragile and distracted. The fatigue in her blue eyes concerned him. He kindly suggested that she take off a personal day from school to rest. When at last she had a positive pregnancy test, it took a while for Mary to believe the news. To her delight, her gestation was remarkably easy and free of morning sickness. It was a full-term pregnancy, and she had plenty of time to fantasize about how beautiful and intelligent her baby would be.

But after her water broke early in the morning of January 25, 1976, Mary had no contractions. She spent the entire day reading magazines and waiting anxiously at the maternity ward of the local hospital. She felt relieved when a sympathetic doctor gave her an epidural to induce labor that evening. Even after her contractions started, however, the fetus seemed stuck and did not move down the birth canal until the doctor resorted to using forceps. The monitors revealed that fetal heartbeat stopped briefly, and the attending nurse expressed concern that the umbilical cord was wrapped around the baby's neck. In the midst of her exhaustion Mary felt panic-stricken. Would she lose the child whom she had dreamed of mothering?

When the infant was finally born on January 26, after twenty-one hours of labor, the six-pound girl had a bruise on her head from the forceps. But, in a brief glimpse before her baby was taken to an oxygen tank in the intensive care unit, Mary thought her long-awaited child Twyla looked lovely. Hours later, when she was permitted to have some physical contact, the inexperienced parent did not notice that the baby lay rigidly in her arms, without cuddling. Because she was planning to return to teaching after a six-month maternity leave, Mary had decided

to bottle-feed her daughter, and she took medicine to dry up her nat-
ural milk supply. But her nurses had trouble stimulating the newborn's
sucking response. When they attempted to feed her formula, Twyla
vomited whatever she ingested. She was diagnosed with lactose intoler-
ance. But at the time that Mary brought her pretty week-old baby
home from the hospital, nobody expected any serious developmental
problems.

When she was three weeks old, Twyla's maternal grandparents visited
and brought her a musical stuffed animal in the form of a little lamb
that played the Brahms "Lullaby." This became the baby's regular day-
time companion. She also found it soothing to rock in a wind-up
swing that played a lilting tune. As a toddler, she enjoyed switching the
dial on a brightly colored Fisher Price toy radio, which played a series
of popular children's tunes. To her mother, the blue-eyed child with
curly blond hair looked like a tiny ballerina, twirling gracefully in her
favorite pale pink leotards.

Because of Twyla's musical inclinations, it came as a shock to Mary
when her day care provider, an experienced mother with five children,
voiced concerns that the nine-month-old child had auditory problems.
Louise reported that Twyla had not reacted when the car door slammed
loudly directly behind her. Even before that, Mary had discounted the
fact that Twyla's only brief instance of babbling—at four months old—
had been disrupted by a serious ear infection accompanied by a high
fever. Although the infant had delighted her mother by producing a
sound like "mama," she made no further attempts to babble. Mary also
remembered suppressing her misgivings at a parade on the Fourth of
July. During canon shots to celebrate the two-hundredth anniversary of
the signing of the Declaration of Independence, her little girl had
watched serenely while other children sobbed and covered their ears
because of the explosions. Twyla could not be deaf, could she?

After being scared into scheduling an audiology exam, Mary wished
her own ears could have blocked the doctor's words: "Your daughter
has no usable hearing in either ear. Here is the address for the American
School for the Deaf, where she can start learning sign language." Mary
was so dazed that she was unable to tell her parents the sad news for
weeks. Jack was devastated to hear that he had a deaf child. When a
subsequent audiogram at the age of eleven months revealed that she
had significant loss but some usable hearing, Twyla started to wear a
body aid, a hearing aid strapped to her chest. To help her toddler look
as normal as possible, Mary sewed pockets on every one of her child's

shirts and dresses so that the device would be unobtrusive. She made sure that Twyla's clothing was clean and neat and that her flaxen hair was nicely combed and tied with pretty ribbons.

Ellen, an energetic early intervention therapist, began to visit once a week and provided activities to stimulate the one-year-old to communicate. She observed that Twyla needed no coaching to hold her miniature radio against the receiver of her hearing aid so that she could appreciate the music. Whenever Mary played her favorite Barbra Streisand records on the stereo, the child would listen intently; at twenty months of age, she hummed some of the pitches of the melodies. Not only would she join her mother in playing simple duets on a pair of toy xylophones, but she would also attempt to copy short rhythmic patterns on a small drum. Despite not learning to walk until she was nineteen months old, the toddler enjoyed dancing with her mother at family wedding receptions and was able to move in rhythm with the music. While visiting a local fair, her expression of pure joy confirmed that she could hear the marching band performing nearby. From Mary's reports and her own observations, it was apparent to the therapist that Twyla could not only hear selected sounds, but that she was also highly motivated to use whatever hearing was intact.

At Ellen's recommendation, Mary started to name familiar objects for her daughter. While pushing the baby carriage around the grocery store, she would label and encourage Twyla to imitate the names of every fruit and vegetable that they encountered. Other shoppers would stare at the lively woman selecting an apple and repeating its name like a mantra until her small companion would echo "abbah." At home, Mary would sketch flowers, trees, and people with brightly colored magic markers, labeling each picture. As she drew, Twyla would place her small hand atop her mother's to sense the forms and letters kinesthetically. These lessons laid the foundation for the child's ongoing interest in art. Her attraction to the color turquoise was so strong that she learned to say the word: she would request her favorite marker for the painstaking task of printing her first name. Whenever Mary wrote the names of the days of the week and the months of the year, she would entice her daughter to join her in reciting the words in sequence. Together they spent countless hours in building vocabulary.

Although she never brought Twyla to the Congregational Church services she attended on Sunday mornings, Mary noted early on that her daughter had many interests of a spiritual nature that set her apart from other children. Whenever her mother recited the Lord's Prayer or the Twenty-Third Psalm, Twyla would listen attentively. On walks down the country road near their house, she enjoyed participating in a ritual of tossing a penny from a bridge into the water below—one for each blessing that Mary would send to absent family members. During one walk, when the two of them encountered a dead rabbit on the roadside, the little girl resisted her mother's attempts to shield her from the corpse and murmured solemnly, "All gone."

Twyla hardly ever slept straight through a night, and she was especially stimulated by the full moon. When moonbeams streamed across her crib, she would stay awake for hours, vocalizing and waving one forefinger delicately in front of her eyes to interact with the light. The world of nature fascinated the child. Outside, she loved to gaze up at stars and to examine flowers or snowflakes in minute detail. On family summer vacations to a lake in New Hampshire, she would play happily on the sandy beach and in the clear water from dawn till dusk, only stopping to take in the beauty of sunrises and sunsets. Inside, she would follow shifting patterns of sunlight on the rug in her bedroom. Her mother's houseplant collection of begonias and ferns intrigued her, and she regularly checked on the growth of each plant. Watching the shadows of trees blowing in the wind outside her bedroom window seemed to soothe her. The first time her parents left Twyla behind during an overnight trip, her maternal grandmother calmed the child's inconsolable crying by holding her up to the window to watch the movements of the trees. Grandma intuitively played classical organ music to help her granddaughter relax so she could go to sleep.

From the moment she woke up, at around 5:30 in the morning, until she fell asleep, Twyla was constantly seeking sensory stimulation. When she was nearly a year old, she was mesmerized by her first exposure to Christmas candles. One of the first words that she attempted to say was "candle." At a later birthday, her mother recalls, Twyla grinned at the six candles on her cake as if she could imagine no better gift. Mary received her own gift at that party: watching her child holding a hand up to one ear to indicate that she could hear the family singing "Happy Birthday." Twyla found bathing almost as pleasurable as light-gazing, and she developed an extended evening ritual of soaking and swishing in the bathtub. After bathing, when Mary would brush and blow-dry her long blond hair, Twyla luxuriated in the calming sensation. Because she liked sensing light pressure on her head, the child began to collect hats and to wear them inside and outside. Going on car rides gave her special enjoyment. If she noticed her mother preparing to leave the house, Twyla would say, "Bye, bye—car," in hopes that she could sit in the passenger seat with the window down and feel the motion of driving as the wind blew through her hair. One of her preferred destinations was a merry-go-round, whose rotating movement and musical accompaniment thrilled her. At home, a favorite ritual involved blowing up balloons and batting them around the house. Every Friday night, when Mary took her to the supermarket, Twyla would make sure that a bag of balloons ended up in the shopping cart. The family became used to navigating around colorful balloons floating in the corners of every room.

Even more than balloons, however, Twyla loved books. She carried books with her wherever she went. Her literary selections varied from simple to sophisticated and covered a wide range of topics. Before the age of two, she would sit and flip through the pages of children's Golden Reader books as her schoolteacher mother read her the captions to the pictures. Mary recalls her four-year-old daughter clutching a new doll and looking through a book that listed female names. When the little girl pointed to "Darcie," her mother said the name out loud. Twyla smiled at her doll, who has been called Darcie ever since. But despite her daughter's precocious interest in literature, Mary found it hard to believe that the barely verbal child could read.

By the time she was two-and-a-half, when she began an intensive educational program called Project Learn, Twyla was an intellectually curious child with many of the repetitive and unusual behaviors associated with autism. She would pace back and forth, nodding her head and occasionally spinning around. She refused all nourishment except for soft baby food and rice cakes smeared with peanut butter or applesauce. Although she would respond to adult attention, she did not interact with her peers and preferred isolated activities. Her three Project Learn instructors concentrated on teaching Twyla and her four language-delayed classmates manual signs and communication skills. By age four, her behavioral reactions showed that she understood basic oral instructions and that she recognized written letters and familiar words; but she seldom spoke or used sign language spontaneously. She was still not toilet trained and needed her diaper changed four or five times a day.

Between the ages of four and twelve, Twyla attended a private school for children with autism and pervasive developmental disorders. There her inattentive behavior and random pointing so interfered with taking standardized tests that she was evaluated as severely mentally retarded.

At that time, although she would say "yes," her expression of negation involved biting one of her hands. If she felt excited and happy, Twyla tended to squeeze both hands together and shake them in front of her face. Despite her limited expressive vocabulary, the child had created gestures that clearly conveyed her feelings. In the school's individualized behavioral program, she learned to sit still for more than thirty seconds at a time, to make eye contact with her teachers, to approximate the sounds of vowels and consonants, and to count single-digit numbers. She seemed to enjoy the physical release of bowling and swimming, and the excitement of watching basketball games. But in between her structured academic lessons and sports events, she retreated to the bathroom for water play or to the gymnasium to bounce a rubber ball around by herself. While she was engaged in these solitary pursuits, her dreamy blue eyes seemed focused inwardly on private thoughts.

Twyla frustrated her teachers by removing her uncomfortable hearing aids whenever possible, but she seemed to perform just as well without them. In fact, when she was wearing the aids, she hummed to herself continuously, indicating that she was receiving too much stimulation. As part of her auditory training program at school, she was asked to identify which of a group of small percussion instruments was being played beneath a table. She was obtaining a perfect score on this test until the speech therapist noticed that the youngster was tricking her by peeking under the table. Her impatient examiner did not realize that Twyla was familiar with more sophisticated musical instruments than those used in the evaluation. At home, the child enjoyed making random sounds on a Casio electronic keyboard and pushing the demonstration button on an electronic organ so that she could listen to programmed music. A newcomer observing her obvious delight in producing musical sounds would not have suspected that she had a hearing impairment.

As much as she loved her daughter and tried to anticipate her needs, Mary was under mounting stress with her full-time teaching position and futile attempts to hold together her failing marriage. She felt isolated and frightened by her husband's ever-increasing mood swings and episodes of violent behavior. Aside from regular weekend dinners with her in-laws and occasional visits from her own elderly parents, the family never socialized. When Jack made disparaging remarks about Twyla being "a bad girl" or "stupid," Mary felt helpless to protect her daughter, who had started to destroy property and to become self-abusive by banging her head on walls and biting herself.

At school, Twyla began having regular toileting accidents and brief seizure-like episodes of losing contact with her surroundings. After a year of prescribing Depakote to control suspected seizures, her doctor found no irregular EEG activity and discontinued the medication; but he expressed concern about her high level of anxiety. During a brief trial of Mellaril to control her anxiety, she vomited so much that her doctor stopped giving her any drugs. But by then, Twyla had developed a nervous habit of twisting clumps of her hair so that she often looked unkempt. With the start of menstruation, her screams and temper tantrums accelerated around the time of each menstrual cycle. Because her teachers could no longer handle her aggressive outbursts, Twyla was transferred back to Project Learn, this time into a class of adolescents with behavioral disorders.

By the time her daughter was fourteen, Mary was so overwhelmed by the deteriorating situations at home and at school that she scheduled the teenager for a sixty-day assessment at a local psychiatric institute. There, through a strict behavior modification program, Twyla learned to stop using her fingers to gobble food and to eat with a fork and spoon. Since she appeared to relax in response to the institute's regular daily schedule, tight structure and clear expectations, she needed no medication other than pills to alleviate her premenstrual syndrome. At the end of the two-month evaluation period, her psychiatric team arranged for her to live at a nearby regional center for mentally retarded and autistic clients and to enter the same school that Jerry and Scott were attending. Once her daughter was safely settled, Mary finally marshaled the strength to leave her husband. It took three more years to finalize their divorce.

In the midst of her parents' stormy separation, Twyla moved to a group home supported by the Connecticut Department of Mental Retardation. In this intermediate care facility, several caretakers assisted her and five other young adults with tending to hygiene, changing clothing, and preparing meals. Despite her resistance to this change in residence, Twyla seemed happy at school because her youthful class-room teacher, Michelle, was very sensitive to her needs. Although she could still repeat the programmed recitations that her mother had taught her, Twyla's functional speech was limited to a few stock phrases such as: "I want juice please," or "I want walk," or "Go bathroom." Her articulation was severely delayed, so her words sounded indistinct. But it was obvious to Michelle that her new student's internal and receptive language skills were highly developed. The teacher adapted a series of short academic lessons to Twyla's quick tempo and short attention span and praised her enthusiastically for using the bathroom appropriately. Instead of confiscating the magazines that the girl carried to and from school, Michelle read articles to her that were appropriate for teenagers. Like normal adolescent girls, Twyla enjoyed receiving "beauty tips" about how to style her hair and paint her nails, and she began to take more pride in her appearance. Also, like many teenagers, she did not like to share her teacher's attention with her four classmates, whom she ignored unless social contact was unavoidable. Although she would join the group for art activities and for walks outside, she kept a safe distance. When she discovered her student's attraction to music, Michelle asked me to include Twyla in a small music therapy group with the objective of fostering some pleasurable interactions with other students.

When Twyla entered my music room for the first time, she was vocalizing to herself and clutching a magazine to her chest. Paying no attention to her three classmates, she brushed past me impulsively and grabbed a bongo drum from a selection of musical instruments. As she started to strike the drum, I played a greeting song on the piano and did my best to match her quick rhythmic pulse. Twyla grinned to acknowledge our musical contact, but she made it clear that she had no interest in stopping drumming at the song's conclusion. She was even less interested in waiting while her classmates took turns choosing instruments. When I took away the bongo drums, her form of protest was to remove her hearing aids and hurl them onto the floor, and to hide her face in the pages of her magazine. Only during her own turns would Twyla emerge from her self-imposed exile to chose a series of sturdy percussion instruments. Regardless of the tempo or dynamics of my accompaniment, she played loudly and rapidly. The instant I finished the farewell song and dismissed the group, she ran out of the room, far ahead of the other students.

Over the following months, Twyla and I had a test of wills. Acting as if she were the only person in the music room, she would bounce out of her seat every few minutes to fetch instruments that attracted her. She sulked and looked insulted when I asked a teacher's aide to help her stay seated between turns. At first, she resisted my rule that her magazines had to remain beneath her chair during music sessions; but as she watched me demonstrating new instruments with intriguing sounds, Twyla had less reason to retreat. Gradually, she learned that she could perform second run-throughs on instruments only when she followed my cues to stop playing. After I praised her classmates for adapting their drumming to my dramatic changes in tempo and dynamics on the piano, she began to moderate the speed and volume of her own playing. My obvious delight at her capacity for self-control made her smile. I began to request that when she finished drumming along with the greeting song, she pass the bongos to one of her classmates. At first she averted her face and shoved the instrument in the direction of the student sitting next to her; but after many rehearsals, sharing instruments became an expected routine. Twyla even looked pleased when her peers would offer her a turn on their instruments. The next step was to tempt her to join her classmates in short and simple instrumental accompaniments to familiar songs. Once each student had learned to shake a tambourine up high and then tap it three times down low, I asked them to play tambourine duets, coordinating their movements with the lyrics: "Shaaaake the tambourine, one, two three!" With much practice, a tambourine ensemble evolved.

Whenever I noticed the slightest improvement in Twyla's social interaction, I gave her praise and attention. Her progress, however, was uneven, with discouraging periods of regression. On days when she was feeling sick or stressed, Twyla had no desire and probably no capacity to sit still or to control her screams. At such times, I would send her to a quiet room to lie in a comfortable beanbag chair, away from stimulating lights and sounds. In early 1992, I began questioning the impact of music therapy sessions on the quality of Twyla's life.

Just then, I heard about a new method of communication called Facilitated Communication, known as FC. I had no inkling that FC would change the circumstances of Twyla, Scott and Jerry's lives. Not only their lives but also my own worldview would be irrevocably altered.

CHAPTER FOUR

Breakthrough: Facilitated Communication

In September of 1992, one of Jerry's teachers brought a Tandy laptop computer to our music therapy session. As I watched in disbelief, she supported his dominant left hand with one hand and pressed the space bar between words with her other—while Jerry typed slowly and carefully with one finger. After waiting in suspense for him to finish his message, I read on the computer screen, "GINGER I LOVE MUSIC WE DANCE VERY WELL TOGETHER CAN WE DANCE FFOR LONGER PERIODS OF TIME." Stunned and moved, I watched as Jerry continued to type in this laborious fashion. Despite a lack of punctuation and occasional misspellings, his written words clearly expressed his interest in George Gershwin's music and a desire to visit a local music library.

Thus I began my first conversation with this man whose intellect, empathy and sense of humor I had greatly underestimated. While I was adjusting to the realization that I could ask him more than "yes" or "no" questions and that our relationship was outgrowing the confines of our music therapy sessions, Jerry typed, "I AM SO HONORED TO HAVE YOU AS A FRIEND AND TEACHER JERRY LOVES YOU VERY MUCH AND I AM SEEING THE RESULTS OF YOUR TRUST IN OTHERS LIKE WE HAVE ALL PRAYED FOR." I was so overwhelmed by this message that I began crying. Jerry noticed my tears and typed, "DONT CRY BE HAPPY SEEING YOU CRY HURTS ME CAN WE TALK EACH TIME I COME." It took me months to process this mind-boggling initiation to Facilitated Communication.

FC was developed in the late 1960s by Rosemary Crossley, an Australian special educator. Intended for people who have few or no means of communication, it is a method that allows them to express themselves in writing. With the help of a 'facilitator,' the student selects letters and forms words on an alphabet board, typewriter, or computer keyboard. The facilitator—a teacher or therapist trained to provide physical assistance—supports the student's wrist, hand or elbow, thus helping to alleviate the effects of poor motor control. Over time, the facilitator aims to gradually withdraw physical support, so that eventually the student may spell out words independently.

The technique has generated great controversy internationally among autism researchers, some of whom believe that, consciously or unconsciously, the facilitators are manipulating students' hands to guide their spelling. Some critics of the practice doubt that students with autism could learn to read without formal education. Others complain that parents' hopes are being raised and then cruelly dashed when their child with autism demonstrates no literacy that can be proven. Indeed, most double-blind studies that have tested the efficacy of FC have had disappointing results. The successful typing that students seem to be able to do with the support of familiar facilitators in the relaxed atmosphere of their home or classroom has not been duplicated when they try typing with unfamiliar facilitators in test situations. FC pioneer Dr. Douglas Biklen of Syracuse University has had to qualify his initial optimistic claims that nearly all nonverbal individuals with autism possess hidden literacy. What seems more likely is that people labeled autistic—like those who are considered normal—encompass a gamut of low to high receptive language skills.

After years of practice, some individuals with autism have been weaned completely from physical touch, so that they can type without support. The accuracy of their typing seems to be influenced by mood and fatigue. Many of these independent typists write that they learned to read on their own by watching television or by observing a parent teaching their normal siblings to read and write. Some autistic typists who still need physical support use unique phonetic spellings that remain consistent— regardless of who is facilitating their typing. These students often mention names, places, or events about which the facilitator has no knowledge at the time but that can be verified later. Advocates of FC have been keeping careful documentation of any such evidence that nonverbal typists—not their facilitators—are the authors of messages that have been produced during FC sessions.

Reports such as these are prompting a fundamental redefinition of autism. Dr. Biklen suggests that in some cases the condition, rather than involving a cognitive deficit, may entail a praxis, which refers to a motor problem with speaking or articulating words or ideas [Biklen, 1993, p. 17]. Classic definitions of autism have not taken into account the possibility that, in certain cases, motor difficulties might outweigh cognitive impairments. Some individuals who are labeled autistic may resemble intelligent stroke victims, frustrated by their inability to convey through words their thoughts, feelings, and aspirations. In an extensive literature review, Anne Donnellan, a professor of education at the University of Wisconsin-Madison, and Martha Leary, a speech and language pathologist from Toronto, found that autism has many characteristics in common with Tourette's syndrome and Parkinson's disease: all three conditions involve difficulty with "starting, stopping, combining, executing, continuing and switching movements" [Donnellan and Leary, 1995, p. 35]. These researchers hypothesize that, in addition to affecting an autistic person's actions and postures, such movement disturbances may disrupt their "speech, images, thoughts, perceptions, memories, and emotions" [Donnellan and Leary, 1995, p. 35].

The acclaimed motion picture *Awakenings*, based on a neurological study by Dr. Oliver Sacks, depicts how the use of either musical rhythms or physical touch can impel Parkinsonian patients to move from frozen postures. For people with autism, the element of physical touch in FC may counter motor problems that are similar to those of patients with Parkinson's disease, and thus encourage them to undertake the movements required for typing. In his eloquent book *Out of Silence,* Russell Martin refers to the research of neurobiologist Philip Lieberman, who found a high correlation between speech deficits and an inability to regulate intricate movements of the hands and fingers; people who cannot speak or who have difficulty speaking tend to have problems using their hands [Martin, 1994/1995, p. 227]. Lieberman's colleague William Calvin has pinpointed a neural network that links a site in the brain's left temporal lobe, the site that dictates motor-sequencing of the hands and arms, with an associated site that manages movements of the oral muscles [Martin, 1994/1995, p. 227].

Flaws in the neural circuits that normally connect the basal ganglia with the prefrontal cortex can disrupt the initiation of all kinds of movements, from pointing a finger to pronouncing a word [Martin, 1994/1995, p. 246]. It is probable that many people with autism have abnormalities in *both* these key parts of the brain. In a 1992 issue of the *American Journal of Psychiatry,* Dr. Joseph Piven of the Department of Psychiatry at John Hopkins School of Medicine reported the results of his examination of the brains of autistic subjects. Using Magnetic Resonance Imaging (MRI), Piven photographed the cortices of thirteen young males with autism and of thirteen matched controls. Seven of the cortices of the men with autism had aberrant creases and perforations, while all those of the control subjects looked normal [Martin, 1994/1995, p. 247]. Although the term 'autism' seems to include several distinct disorders, it is evident that neurological problems with speech and motor control affect many of those labeled 'autistic.'

Russell Martin points out that language acquisition "does not appear to be dependent on expressive practice" [Martin, 1994/1995, p. 244]. He discusses his autistic nephew's facility with FC, despite difficulty articulating more than isolated words. Martin explains that by listening to speech, his nephew Ian had acquired internal language without the ability to vocalize it [Martin, 1994/1995, p. 244]. He surmises that Ian's brain is damaged in its motor centers, but that his receptive language centers are intact.

Like Ian, Jerry was able to convey in written form mature grammar and syntax that he could not communicate in spoken words. And, like Ian, he manifested some of the behavioral changes that often accompany newfound self-expression with FC. Once he could type, Jerry had progressively fewer temper tantrums. His attention span increased to two hours of conversation at a sitting. Any doubt that I might have had that he was the author of these typed messages dissipated over the next few months. When he was engaged in dialogue, he would regularly offer his arm to the facilitator to indicate his wish to respond. Jerry's artwork was congruent with his typed communications. His choice of topics, sophisticated vocabulary, and sense of humor were consistent with several different facilitators. It was only when he was tired or upset that his movement disturbance appeared to worsen, resulting in perseveration on certain letters. During a half hour interview with Jerry in October of 1993, Dr. Oliver Sacks was impressed by the congruence between Jerry's behavior and the content of his typed comments. Partly on the basis of their meeting, the neurologist has resisted pressure to take a public stance against the validity of FC.

My first attempts to facilitate Jerry were unsuccessful. I found it difficult to pull back his hand steadily after he struck each key on the computer. With an experienced facilitator supporting his wrist, Jerry consoled me by typing, "TRY EACH TIME WE GET TOGETHER TRY HARD GINGER I AM NOT EASY TO FACILITATE." After several weeks of practice, I managed to assist Jerry enough so that we could converse. Although he lost no time in asking my permission to play the piano, he never reproached me for the years that I had offered him only simple percussion instruments and resonator bells. He graciously accepted my apologies for underestimating his abilities, and we moved into new musical territory together. After having an opportunity to warm up his stiff and poorly coordinated fingers with a delicate improvisation on the black piano keys, Jerry typed that he wanted me and a teacher's aide to accompany him on drums and tambourine. When I played him a tape recording of our first jam session, he was so pleased that he typed a name for our ensemble: "THE TREAT TRIO."

I realized that some of my colleagues who were staunch disbelievers in the validity of FC could not accept the possibility that they might have been boring their students. For me, embracing FC meant admitting that for years I had wrongly assessed the capabilities of students I had grown to love. I felt lucky to be working in a school whose open-minded administrators provided teacher training sessions, so that every student could have opportunities to try FC. Over time, it became obvious that while some had no inclination or ability to type, others welcomed the chance to express what they had been thinking and feeling during many years of silence. Like normal people, individuals classified as autistic have cognitive abilities ranging from severe mental retardation to high intelligence. Some of those who had been labeled retarded were now demonstrating that they were cognitively astute.

Even more than Jerry, Scott proved challenging for me to facilitate. I watched his teacher facilitating him as he punched his left forefinger at his keyboard with quick, jerky movements, often overshooting the letters he intended to type. Since his messages contained a large number of typographical errors, I could decipher his communications most easily when I observed what letters he had missed with his faulty aim. I doubted my ability to assist such an erratic typist. But after months of our relying on others to facilitate him in music sessions, Scott wrote the following message: "DOO TIBPE WIT H DDB ANHD CT GI NGBVER V YES B Y ES." His facilitator translated out loud: "DO TYPE WITH DAD AND CANT GINGER YES YES." Shamed by the news that his father was making an effort to facilitate him, I supported Scott's left hand and did my best to follow his motions while watching where he was aiming. To my astonishment, he spelled out, "6YTEZS BREST WEASS5RWED BTHSTD GYHOUVB CJNM VD9O IT." If I had not witnessed his composing process, I would have dismissed the series of letters as gobbledygook instead of detecting the following message: "YES REST ASSURED THAT YOU CAN DO IT." It was obvious that although I had been trying to hide my trepidation, Scott sensed I needed reassurance as a facilitator. This was among the first of many times that I wondered "Who's teaching whom?" Once I felt confident enough to facilitate him without supervision, I decided that for validation purposes I would type all my own verbalizations and note Scott's significant behaviors and choices of instruments, so that by the end of each music therapy session there would be a complete transcript. After each of Scott's comments I added in parentheses a cleaned-up version, free of typographical mistakes, so that I could easily review the sequence of our interchanges. (With a few rare and obvious exceptions, subsequent FC excerpts have been edited for legibility.)

During one memorable joint music and language session, his speech therapist Jamie facilitated Scott typing a messy approximation of "I AM SMART." As I improvised a song about how smart he was, the boy grinned. Like many autistic individuals who were starting to express themselves through FC, Scott sought recognition for an intelligence that had been hidden and unacknowledged for too long. He went on to type, "I WANT TO TALK." Stifling my doubts, I experimented with an adapted form of "melodic intonation therapy," which has helped some aphasic people recover their speech in the aftermath of strokes. I asked Scott to hum a tune. While he was intoning a high-pitched minor third, Jamie remembered that, as a toddler, he had been able to say the word "cookie." Using the same two pitches as his humming, I sang "cookie." Carefully watching my mouth, Scott contorted his lips and bravely tried to copy my sounds. After many false attempts, he managed to articulate "cookie" clearly enough that Jamie and I both cheered and applauded. Although he was exhausted by his efforts and unable to duplicate his success, the heroic singer had proven that he could indeed talk. This demonstration seemed to satisfy him, and Scott did not pursue speaking in subsequent sessions. Later on, when he was attending classes with normal children in a local public school, he typed that talking had been "TOO HARD," and that he had learned to accept FC as his primary form of communication.

Like Jerry, Scott demonstrated more self-control and fewer tantrums once he could express his thoughts and feelings through FC. One day he typed to me, "HATE BEING CAN'T I HATE IT WHEN I CAN'T DO STUFF." In response to this expression of frustration, I asked, "Would you like to get some hate out on the drum?" Scott signed "Yes," and used a set of drumsticks to beat a standing drum fast and furiously. When his beloved classroom teacher gave him two months notice that she would be leaving to work in another school, he vented his sadness and anger during his next music session by typing, "MAD REAL FRIENDS DONT GO" and "WISH I COULD GO TOO." This time drumming hard did not seem to help. Scott lamented, "HEAD HURTS NO TOO MUCH BAD FEELING" and then lay his forehead on the piano keyboard. He appeared to relax as I rocked him and sang a song about the sadness of separating from friends, but he needed a series of sessions to absorb this personal loss so soon after his parents' divorce. In fact, he requested repeated renditions of a song I had improvised at the time his parents separated: "Scotty Misses His Mom Today." I was touched by his reaching out to me for support and his ability to articulate painful emotions instead of screaming in solitude as he had done in the past.

As his behavior improved enough for him to attend a class several times a week in public school, Scott communicated, "I WANT TO PLAY BETTER ON PIANO." Although his teacher told me that he had showed off, performing "Mary Had a Little Lamb" for his new classmates, Scott typed, "I WANT A SONG FROM THE RADIO EVERYONE AT SCHOOL WILL KNOW." He was expressing an understandable adolescent desire to fit in with his peer group. When I suggested that he try learning the popular song "Every Breath You Take" by the rock star "Sting," Scott wrote, "TOO HARD I HATE PRACTICE WANT TO PLAY EASY WITH NO WORK." But after I asked how he mastered "Mary Had a Little Lamb," he smiled sheepishly and admitted, "PRACTICE I KNOW." His initial resistance gave way to dedicated rehearsals. I placed color-coded stickers on the four piano keys involved in the new melody and guided his left forefinger with my hand until he began to sense the kinesthetic pattern. Even though I weaned him slowly from my touch, Scott found it difficult to switch directions in order to play a descending line once he had started an ascending one, and vice versa. His whole body looked rigid with strain as he struggled to control the unpredictable movements of his left hand. Throughout months of music sessions, he persevered until he could play the chorus part of Sting's hit tune on both the piano and resonator bells. He solved the problem of how to deal with the daunting technical difficulty of the song's verses by humming them in between renditions of the chorus on the keyboard.

Because of the enormity of his efforts to mix with normal classmates, Scott appreciated breaks from public school. One day he typed to me, "I LIKE SCHOOL BUT IT IS HARD TO BE AUTISTIC I HAVE SHOULDER PAIN I HATE PAIN IN MY SHOULDERS I NEED HELP TENSE FROM SCHOOL." Responding to his clear description of his physical and emotional state, I incorporated a "Back Scratching Song" into our repertoire and recommended that he receive massages from a physical therapist. When Scott wrote that he was trying hard to restrain his vocal noises in school, I assured him that it was appropriate to make such sounds in music sessions. After happily humming the melodies to some of his favorite tunes, he picked a whistle and blew it as hard as possible to activate a loud siren. He blared the wind instrument for such a long time that I asked him how his head was feeling. His triumphant response was, "GOOD EVEN THOUGH I CANT TALK I CAN MAKE SOUNDS." The combination of music therapy and FC was ideal for Scott's mixture of nonverbal and verbal self-expression.

In the fall of 1994, Scott took part in a FC validation study that was intended to alleviate any doubts about the authorship of his typed messages. During the various trials of the experiment, a facilitator would encourage him to choose a photograph from several magazines and to type comments about its content. Once this task was accomplished, the facilitator would leave the room with a printed copy of Scott's typing, after erasing any evidence from his computer. Then a naïve facilitator would join Scott and ask him open-ended questions about the content of the message he had just typed. The second communication was compared with the first. Although Scott failed to give accurate reports on some occasions, the fact that he did so in other instances proved that he could indeed convey information to a facilitator who knew nothing about it beforehand.

Twyla's eccentric typing style, like Scott's, caused observers unfamiliar with FC to doubt that she was the author of her messages. She tended to strike each computer key forcefully and rapidly and to drag her left forefinger downward over several adjacent keys. As one of her facilitators, I had to remind her repeatedly to "slow down and relax your wrist" or "stop dragging your finger." What motivated me to persevere was watching Twyla's self-esteem grow as FC enabled her to communicate the creative ideas she had bottled up since early childhood. Now she could prepare for entering one of her paintings in a "Very Special Arts" show by selecting peach-colored matting and a gold frame. Through typing, she explained that her choices enhanced the bright primary colors and strong lines of her floral design. Twyla wrote that her work of art should be titled "Outrageous Thought." With her posture more erect and her head held higher than usual, she looked proud to have her artistry acknowledged. As she experienced the satisfaction of actualizing some of her dreams, she had fewer tantrums and better control of her impulses.

When we incorporated FC into her music therapy sessions, Twyla began by spelling brief comments such as "NO NMORE DRUM" or "COW BELL" or "TAMBORIUNER" to indicate her choice of musical instruments. I had no trouble reading her requests because she made few typographical mistakes. Once she sensed my growing more comfortable with the rhythm of her typing, she made a concerted effort to write complete sentences to express her thoughts and feelings. As her messages increased in complexity, they did so as well in spelling errors. Communicating that she was feeling tense and anxious about plans for her to attend several classes a week with normal high school students, Twyla asked if I could bring recordings of "RELAXING MUSIC TO HELP ME CALM DOWN." At that point, I realized that she had outgrown the confines of her music group, and I scheduled her for individual music therapy sessions. Alone in the music room with me for the first time, she typed excitedly that she and Jerry had been invited to join a "FACILITATED COMMUNICATION SUPPORT GROUP."

I discovered that my colleague, Gene, a local social worker, had been so impressed by the facilitated messages of some of his nonverbal clients that he had founded a group therapy program for five young autistic adults, including Twyla and Jerry. Every two weeks the participants and their facilitators would arrive with laptop computers for an hour-long meeting. When I visited as an observer, I was struck by how the format was similar to that of traditional psychotherapy groups. Gene, an attractive balding man with decades of therapeutic experience, led the group in a kindly and respectful manner. His gentle sense of humor and supportive comments made him easy to trust. He started off by asking the participants if they had any issues they wanted to discuss. The group members, each with a facilitator nearby, sat typing in a circle so that they could all see one another. Without interpreting, the facilitators read out loud the content of the typed messages. Gene chose one or two topics that seemed most pressing and moderated a discussion.

Themes that surfaced during the first year that the FC support group met were loneliness, frustration and depression about not being able to speak, fears of abandonment, sexuality, family problems, and difficulties dealing with "NORMAL" people who "REGARD US AS FREAKS," "LAUGH AT US," or "THINK WE ARE STUPID" [Eliasoph and Donnellan, 1995, p. 554]. Although these themes were similar to those discussed in any therapy group, they carried more emotional weight. Most autistic people experience extreme levels of isolation and ostracism.

When Gene examined why group members did not talk, one typed that efforts to speak caused pain in the larynx, another that he could not put words in the right order, and several that they had too little breath control to blow out a candle. Jerry noted, "MY BODY IS OFTEN MY

WORST ENEMY IT DOES DIFFERENT THINGS THAN MY MIND TELLS IT." He expressed a fear of failure and resonated with Twyla's typed comment, "WORDS HURT" [Eliasoph and Donnellan, 1995, p. 557]. This was one of several occasions when group participants thanked Gene for listening to them with respect and for giving them opportunities to establish friendships with fellow autistic adults. They made it clear how much they treasured this opportunity to socialize and to discuss common problems. None of them fit the commonly-held assumption that persons labeled autistic are socially disinterested or emotionally distant. In fact, after Gene incorporated psychodrama into one of the sessions, Twyla typed that she was relieved to receive group support while enacting a scene from her childhood, when she had felt helpless to protect her mother from her father's rage.

During weekly music therapy sessions, Twyla and Jerry kept me informed through FC about events in their group meetings. I noticed that parallel breakthroughs were occurring in both settings. Shortly before participating in a group discussion of dreams, Jerry typed to me, "I DREAMED I WAS NORMAL." His comment was a revelation. He was indicating that he had a capacity to generate internal images—an attribute generally thought to be lacking in people with autism. Jerry's statement galvanized me to adapt a music therapy technique called Guided Imagery and Music (GIM) for his needs.

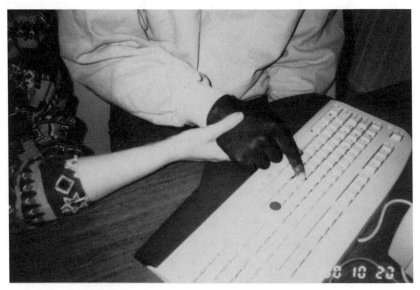

Jerry typing with Facilitated Communication

CHAPTER FIVE

Jerry's Path to Self-Expression

In retrospect, it seems, at the least, a remarkable coincidence that I was completing a three-year training program in GIM just as Jerry began to communicate about his dream life. Developed by music therapist Dr. Helen Bonny in the 1970s, GIM is "a music-centered transformational therapy which uses specifically programmed classical music to stimulate and sustain a dynamic unfolding of inner experiences, in support of physical, psychological, and spiritual wholeness" [Clark and Keiser, 1989]. Because the Bonny method employs music to evoke an inward journey, the roles of therapist and patient or client are referred to, respectively, as 'guide' and 'traveler.' A typical individual GIM session begins with the guide joining in a brief discussion about an issue or theme that the traveler has chosen to explore. During the next phase, the traveler lies down with eyes closed while the guide, speaking in a slow, soft tone of voice, leads an induction exercise to relax the body and focus the mind. Then, from about thirty programs of classical music, the guide selects one to match the client's particular issue and state of mind.

Each program starts at a baseline of musical intensity and complexity, rises to a peak, and provides for a resolution. While listening, the traveler responds to rhythmic changes, melodic curves, and harmonic tension and release points. The music is like a magnet, drawing forth unfinished business from the psyche. It serves as a co-therapist, attracting projections and providing a container for the client's inner explorations. As the music stimulates body sensations, emotions, and images or memories, the client verbally reports inner experiences. The guide asks questions or makes interventions designed to deepen the traveler's connection to whatever is arising. While he is shifting levels of consciousness and entering fully into a waking dream, the client may experience feelings of spinning or seasickness, sensations of falling or flying, and changes in temperature or in perception of space and time. As the music ends, the guide gently talks the traveler back to ordinary consciousness. The client may then integrate musically-evoked symbols, metaphors and insights by having a discussion with the guide and/or by drawing a depiction of the experience within an empty circle, creating a "mandala."

GIM was conceived to help verbal clients with a capacity for free association to resolve psychodynamic issues and to progress on a path of individuation. When I undertook the training program, my goal was to use GIM with normal adults interested in exploring mid-life questions of identity and purpose. It never crossed my mind that any of the autistic students with whom I had been so involved for over two decades could benefit from such a technique. Jerry's report of his dream shocked me into the realization that his mind was encompassing far more than the limited and concrete thoughts that autistic individuals were assumed to have. In his book *The Autistic Child,* I. N. Kugelmass defined the condition as "complete social aphasia with marked CNS (central nervous system) disorgnization. It is a specific syndrome of organic brain disease characterized by a basic inability to transform visual and auditory experience into meaningful patterns for understanding the surrounding world" [Kugelmass, 1970, p. ix]. If he could dream, however, Jerry could remember images from the past and imagine future scenarios. He could indeed "transform visual and auditory experience into meaningful patterns." And, rather than avoiding personal interaction as might be expected if he had "complete social aphasia," he was inviting me to share his dream life.

When I asked if he would be interested in undergoing some relaxation exercises and dreaming to classical music, Jerry responded enthusiastically. In adapting the GIM format to his needs, I used simple inductions and briefer-than-usual musical selections, and I provided ample opportunities for him to draw and type beforehand and afterwards. Although most of the music repertoire was classical, I incorporated some soothing New Age pieces as well.

Because of Jerry's autistic resistance to change, all his GIM sessions had the same basic structure. Instead of the traditional pre-session discussion, he would begin by typing about his current state of mind and an issue that he wanted to explore. We reviewed any major events that had occurred or drawings that he had completed in between sessions. Then he would lie down in the same corner of the music room and close his eyes, while he was covered with a familiar blanket. He listened while I guided him through a simple relaxation exercise. Once he looked relaxed, I would play a cassette tape or compact disc of a single musical selection or a sequence of several short pieces, lasting between five and twenty minutes per session. Rather than using the traditional GIM technique of making verbal or physical interventions to develop reported imagery, I would carefully observe Jerry's nonverbal responses to the music and silently note any body movements or facial expressions, including smiles, twitches, grimaces, and fluttering eyelids. I noticed when he appeared agitated and when he seemed calm. As soon as I announced that the music had ended, Jerry would jump up and sit at a table where a set of magic markers and an open sketch pad with a pre-drawn circle awaited him. It was his habit to arrange the markers in a straight row, and, with only two exceptions, to use only one color, depending on the mood induced by the music. After creating a mandala (and, if he wished, a free-hand drawing), he would painstakingly print his signature: "JERRY." He ended each GIM session by typing about the musical selection and about his imagery, physical sensations, and emotional reactions. Jerry usually assigned a title to his mandalas and other drawings and discussed their content. Before he left, he nearly always typed an expression of thanks.

Jerry's first GIM series consisted of nineteen sessions, lasting from November 1993 through June 1994. Reviewing the complete transcript of his introductory session reminds me of what unknown territory I was entering. Our preliminary dialogue went as follows:

> Ginger (G): Do you have something that you have been think-
>   ing about for this GIM session?
> Jerry (J): I WANT TO SEE HOW MY MIND WORKS WITH THE MUSIC
> G: Would you like to lie down or sit up as you listen to the music?
> J: I WOULD LIKE TO LIE DOWN
> G: Would you be comfortable closing your eyes while you listen?
> J: I WILL CLOSE MY EYES

Despite more than a year of experience with FC, I had doubts that Jerry would actually carry out the radical changes in routine implied by his typed resolutions, and I was surprised to see him settle down on the floor with his eyes shut.

> G: I will give you a relaxation exercise to help you focus your
>   mind and relax your body. Then I will play eight minutes of
>   classical music. You can draw a mandala in a circle form after
>   the music, and then we can type together about what you have
>   experienced. Does that sound OK?
> J: YES.

For the induction, I suggested that he breathe deeply into each body part. The music selected for this first session was a gentle, structured "Sarabande" from Benjamin Britten's *Simple Symphony*. Jerry's

Fig. 1: Jerry's mandala from initial GIM session

mandala was a sad-looking gray face locked inside a thick circular wall
of red and gray brick (Figure 1). It depicts his experience of autism as
being trapped within the confines of his own mind. During the processing phase, Jerry and I discussed his artwork and his musical journey:

G: Do you have a title for your drawing?

J: I WANT THE TITLE TO BE TRIPPING TO MUSIC

G: I like your title. Could you write about what you felt during
the music?

J: WILD ANIMALS AND TILTING BUILDINGS AND WEIRD SUBJECTS

G: How did you feel about these weird subjects?

J: I FELT GREAT

G: I noticed at one point your feet were moving.

J: THEY WERE RUNNING WITH DEER SEEING DEER GOING SEEING AN
ANIMAL

G: Where were the deer in your imagery?

J: THEY WERE IN A FOREST I DREW MYSELF AND DREW WHAT AUTISM
FEELS LIKE

G: Could you tell me more about what autism feels like for you?

J: EXCITING SOUNDS AND SIGHTS AND SMELLS AND SENSES AND NICE
COLOR

G: How do you feel in your drawing?

J: THE DRAWING IS FEELING DEPRESSED

G: Can you say why he feels that way?

J: BECAUSE HE CANT DO ALL THE THINGS HE DREAMS ABOUT

G: Would you like to try GIM again to see more of how your mind works?

J: YES EACH TIME WE DO GUIDED IMAGERY AND MUSIC I WILL FEEL FREE

The running wild deer that Jerry imaged during his initial GIM session recurred many times as a symbol of freedom. By the fourth session, he dreamed that a buffalo and a snake had joined the deer. When I questioned him about the snake, Jerry typed, "IT TELLS ME THE TRUTH." I asked, "What is the truth?" and he answered, "IT IS THAT I WILL GET BETTER." Another key image was of five friendly (Native American) Indians wearing costumes and feathered headdresses. Jerry wrote that they were making "A TREATY TO TRY TO HELP ME WITH AUTISM THEY SAID THAT I WILL GET BETTER BUT I NEED HELP." After envisioning the Indians again in a subsequent session, he typed, "THEY DREAMED THAT I COULD BE NORMAL." Once he encountered these interior allies, he no longer felt alone in his quest to lead a normal life. During the fifth session, Jerry reported, "I DREAMED THAT THE INDIANS MET ME AND TOLD ME NOT TO WORRY ABOUT AUTISM." At this point in the GIM series, I was touched by the wisdom and shamanic quality of Jerry's music-evoked imagery.

In the sixth session, I was surprised by the following message: "I DREAMED THAT SNAKES WERE COMING TO SEE ME AND THEY TOLD ME I WILL BE FREE TO BE FRED VERY HAPPY DID YOU GET WHAT I SAID." I responded, "I do not understand who Fred is. Please tell me." Jerry's answer was, "FRED IS ME WHEN I WAS SAD HE HAS HOPE THAT HE CAN GET BETTER AND HE CAN LIVE INDEPENDENTLY." During the ninth session, Jerry clarified the "Fred" side of himself: "FRED IS ME WHEN IM SAD AND JERRY IS ME WHEN I AM DREAMING AND WORKING EVERY DAY." With further questioning, Jerry revealed that ever since the age of three, when he felt frustrated by not being able to talk, Fred had been both his inner partner and the source of his compulsions. I felt touched that Jerry trusted me enough to introduce this secret side of himself. But I recognized that the GIM series was uncovering dimensions of Jerry's psyche that would have to be integrated before he could realize his fantasies of living independently.

A truth-telling snake appeared in Jerry's imagery during the fifteenth session, with these messages: "FRED AND THE SNAKE ARE SOUL BROTHERS" and "SNAKE BROTHER IS ALWAYS WITH ME." By that time, Jerry had reported encounters with several wise snakes. In the seventeenth session, he typed that his snake friends had said, "DONT WORRY ABOUT THE FUTURE STAY IN THE PRESENT." The philosophy of these inner animal guides struck me with its similarity to Buddhist religious practice, which also encourages the practitioner to "stay in the present." Back in session seven, Jerry had envisioned three snakes, whom he identified as a father, mother, and child. His freehand drawing depicted the child attached to the father snake (Figure 2). When I asked, "Why is the child not attached to the mother?" Jerry replied, "THE SNAKE NEEDS HER FATHER MORE RIGHT NOW." This image indicated that in his efforts towards more independent living, Jerry was longing for a paternal figure to replace his absent father.

Images of his dad surfaced in the eighth session. As he listened to the male vocal music I had selected, Jerry typed, "I THINK ABOUT FATHERS DEATH AND FEEL SAD." In the aftermath of this session, I phoned Jerry's supervisory team's leader to ask if his father was truly deceased. I learned that his dad was living locally with a second wife and their nine-year-old daughter, neither of whom Jerry had met. Despite sporadic visits beforehand, there had been no contact between father and son for the past four years. In Jerry's mind, his father seemed dead. Before the ninth GIM session, Jerry's residential counselor phoned his father, who expressed an interest in seeing his son. After his imagery reflected the impact of hearing this news, Jerry reported, "I DREAMED THAT DAD CAME TO SEE FRED AND SAID DONT GIVE UP HOPE DAD DANCED

Fig. 2: Jerry's freehand drawing from GIM session #7

WITH FRED AND FRED FEELS HAPPY NOW." Jerry's father was so touched by reports of his son's images about their relationship that he arranged a reunion in February 1994. While facilitating Jerry's typing, I was moved to tears as he reestablished a bond with his father, who shares his love of music and dancing. The resemblance between the two tall, dignified-looking black men was striking.

For all his best intentions, however, Jerry's father did not follow up on that initial visit. Unemployed and feeling torn between his new and old families, he broke several dates with his son and seemed unwilling to assume paternal responsibilities. Jerry's imagery revealed his ambivalence about this unreliable relationship. During the eleventh GIM session, he dreamed, "DAD CAME AND STAYED WITH ME IN THE SAME APARTMENT WHERE DAD USED TO LIVE." When I queried, "Was anyone else living with you?" Jerry responded, "NO JUST DAD AND FRED AND THEY WERE HAPPY." In that same session he typed about feeling "SAD AND FRIGHTENED ABOUT DAD COMING DEAD AND ALIVE AND DEAD AGAIN." Jerry's confusion was painfully apparent. By the fifteenth session several weeks later, he was still express-ing complex emotions about his father: "FRED FEELS SAD AND ANGRY." Here I took an unusually active role, preparing him for imaging to music by suggesting, "Could you let the snakes who tell you the truth speak to you about your dad and about what Fred needs to do right now to grow up and feel more independent and happy?" Jerry's answer was, "YES FRED WILL HEAR THE TRUTH SNAKES SPEAK." After listening to the music, we engaged in an emotional dialogue:

J: I DREAMED ABOUT FRED AND DAD AND THEY WERE FIGHTING ABOUT DAD NOT COMING TO VISIT FRED

G: Did the truth snakes have anything to say?

J: YES THE TRUTH SNAKES SAID DO NOT WAIT FOR DAD TO COME

G: How does Fred feel about that?

J: FRED FEELS SAD BUT FRED KNOWS THAT THE SNAKES ARE RIGHT

G: Fred is growing up and that can feel painful sometimes. What else happened after the fight?

J: FRED SAID DO NOT COME SEE ME UNTIL YOU ARE ABLE TO REALLY BE WITH ME

G: Fred is asserting himself and saying what he needs to Dad. Do the friends around Fred make a difference?

J: YES THEY DECIDE WHETHER FRED WANTS TO DIE OR LIVE AND THEY GIVE FRED HOPE AND THEY DECIDE THAT FRED WILL GROW UP NOW

G: Congratulations, Fred is growing up.

Among the themes central to Jerry's initial GIM series was that of reconnecting and then separating from his father in order to become an independent adult. Shortly after visiting with his father, he sketched an oval within a concentric circle to which a crescent shape was attached (Figure 3). Through pointing and typing, Jerry identified the shapes sequentially as "YOU AND FRED AND DAD ALL TOGETHER."

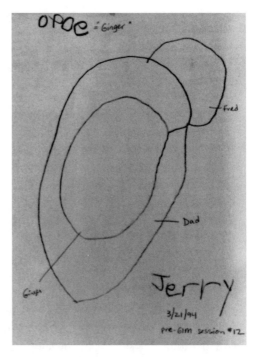

Fig. 3: Jerry's sketch following a visit from his father

En route to individuating, he utilized art to express feelings of attachment to me and to his father. Such psychodynamic work is challenging enough for persons without the perceptual and motor disabilities associated with autism. I was awed by Jerry's ego strength, which enabled him to reach developmental milestones faster than many of my normal clients. His commitment to self-exploration was unshakable and reminded me of his first response to the idea of participating in a GIM session: "I WANT TO SEE HOW MY MIND WORKS WITH THE MUSIC." Even when the inner work involved uncomfortable feelings of loss, betrayal, and anger, Jerry persevered with his quest for self-knowledge. He did not shy away from the hard work of integrating the aspects of himself represented by Fred and Jerry.

The themes of longing for freedom and sadness about living within the limitations of autism were prominent in Jerry's initial GIM series. During the second session he typed, "I AM THINKING ABOUT CARRYING GRIEF ABOUT BEING AUTISTIC" and "I NEED TO LIVE WHERE IT IS QUIET AND CALM." Later, in the nineteenth session, Jerry communicated, "I AM FEELING SILLY AND I DO DISMAY ABOUT ALOT OF COMPULSIONS." His imagery reflected a desire to control such typically autistic compulsions as licking his hands or laughing without reason for long periods of time: "I DREAMED ABOUT SNAKES SAYING STOP COMPULSIONS SO YOU CAN ENJOY

THE MUSIC." Near the end of this session, he resolved, "I WILL TRY TO LIS-
TEN TO MUSIC WHEN I START TO FEEL COMPULSIVE." I gave him some classical music recordings that he could play whenever he felt the need to
channel his energy in a more positive direction. He gave his fifth mandala the title: "FREEDOM TO VISION A NEW FUTURE." One of his memorable quotations from the eighteenth session was, "I DREAMED THAT I WAS
FREE AND NORMAL AND ARTISTIC." My immediate response was, "You are
artistic in real life!"

In June 1994, Dianne, a graphic designer on his supervisory team,
was so impressed by Jerry's artistic talent that she enlisted his help in
starting a greeting card business called "Flew the Coop." His outer life
was beginning to mirror the gains he was making internally, but the
changes were anxiety-provoking. Jerry opened the seventeenth session
by writing, "I WANT FREEDOM FROM STRESS." After listening to the music,
he reported, "I DREAMED THAT I WAS FREE AND DREAMED ABOUT SNAKES
HELPING ME TO RELAX." His GIM sessions assisted him in adapting to the
challenging transition from his former menial jobs of raking leaves or
stuffing envelopes to a creative career in graphic design.

The artwork that Jerry created in conjunction with his GIM series
revealed subtle but significant developmental changes. Because of dis-
liking the sensation of touching pastel color sticks, he drew with magic
markers. The thick border of his initial mandala indicated the heavy
defense system characteristic of people with autism. While he was
drawing this mandala, Jerry showed the intensity of his emotions by
using such heavy pressure on the gray and red markers that the colors
bled through several sheets of paper. Art therapist Joan Kellogg writes in
her book *Mandala: Path of Beauty* that the color combination of red and
gray may symbolize "archetypal guilt related to the hopelessness and
depression connected to the right of one's organism to life. This may
have roots in the struggle for life in the uterine environment" [Kellogg,
1984, p. 39]. It is not surprising that Jerry described his portrayal of the
fortified gray face as "depressed."

Although most of his subsequent mandalas followed the same
basic design of a face within a wall-like mind, they vary in color
choice, thickness of rim, facial expression, and in detail. Despite some
perseveration stemming from the brain damage Jerry sustained due
to oxygen deprivation at birth, his mandalas do not reflect intellec-
tual retardation. His optional freehand drawings depict a variety of
primitive images. In most cases, he wrote clear reasons for selecting
particular colors and shapes. During his second GIM session, Jerry

created a bright blue and green mandala, one of only two that combined colors. Its rim is thinner than that of the first mandala, and the facial expression is happier (Figure 4).

Fig. 4: Jerry's mandala from his second GIM session

Fig. 5: "Freedom to Vision a New Future," Jerry's mandala from GIM session #5

In the subsequent two sessions, Jerry explained his color choices as follows: "RED FEELS BRIGHT AND CHEERFUL" and "YELLOW IS A GLAD COLOR AND I LIKE IT." The facial expression of his fifth mandala includes a smile and raised eyebrows, and the rim no longer appears like a solid wall but rather like a loose-knit web with regular open spaces. The drawing indicated that he no longer felt so trapped within the confines of his own mind (Figure 5). Jerry gave this mandala the title "FREEDOM TO VISION A NEW FUTURE." He brought free-hand drawings to the fourth and fifth sessions. One portrays Jerry with his Indian guides near a teepee; and the other depicts his animal allies, the deer and the buffalo, with big smiles on their faces (Figures 6 and 7). His next drawing showed two "truth snakes" on wheels (Figure 8). When I asked about their unusual shape, Jerry replied humorously that they were "FREE WHEELING SNAKES." Explaining his color choices for the mandalas in sessions six through nine, he typed: "BLUE IS A COLOR THAT IS SAD AND GLAD DOUBLE. . . . BROWN IS A COLOR THAT IS CRUMBY BUT THE FACE IS SMILING IN THE MIDDLE OF THE SHIT. . . . BLACK IS THE COLOR OF DEATH BUT FRED IS SMILING BECAUSE HE CAN BE WITH HIS FATHER IS HIS DREAMS. . . . GREEN IS FREEDOM AND GLADNESS."

Although he had been selecting specific colors to convey various emotional states, the basic format of Jerry's drawings remained the same until the twelfth GIM session, when he drew a mandala that had a startlingly

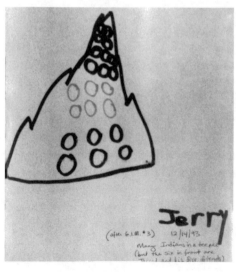

Fig. 6: Jerry and Indian guides near teepee— drawing brought to GIM session #4

different appearance (Figure 9). It portrayed a bright red face outlined by a single thin line. Three circles indicated a nose and eyes below raised eyebrows. The mandala's most striking feature was an open mouth containing upper and lower teeth. Teeth had never before appeared in his mandalas. After he stopped drawing, Jerry commented, "THE HEAD IS FREE AND THE TEETH ARE SMILING FRED FEELS RELIEVED ABOUT ANGER GOING AWAY SO THAT JERRY CAN DREAM AGAIN."

Fig. 7: Smiling deer and buffalo—drawing brought to GIM session #5

The color choice was no accident. "Symbolically in terms of energy for asserting and affirming," writes Kellogg, "red is important" [Kellogg, 1984, p. 35]. It was obvious that this mandala was instrumental in releasing angry feelings towards his father. Interestingly, Jerry's next two freehand drawings were orange-colored depictions of himself dancing with his father. According to Kellogg, large amounts of orange may express hostility to the personal father [Kellogg, 1984, p. 40]. Reflecting on the drawings, Jerry wrote, "ORANGE IS DADS COLOR DAD LIKES ORANGE." Throughout the GIM series, he utilized artwork to convey a wide range of emotions that he could not communicate through speech.

While his art expressed deep parts of Jerry's psyche, the music that I selected for his GIM sessions evoked even deeper elements of his interior life. For his first four sessions, I chose single pieces that are all characterized by an adagio tempo, a gentle mood, and a clear structure. Britten's "Sarabande" from the *Simple Symphony* provided a secure and predictable container for his initial GIM experience. During the second session, after listening to the adagio movement of Beethoven's *Piano Concerto No. 5,* Jerry wrote, "IT WAS BEETHOVEN." He was happy that I had chosen a piece by one of his most beloved composers. In the following two sessions, he recognized Bach as the composer of "Come Sweet Death" and the "Largo" from *Concerto for Two Violins*. Referring to the first Bach piece, he commented, "I LIKED THE CELLO AND THE FEELINGS," and regarding the second one, he stated, "I LIKED THE VIOLINS DANCING TOGETHER." I

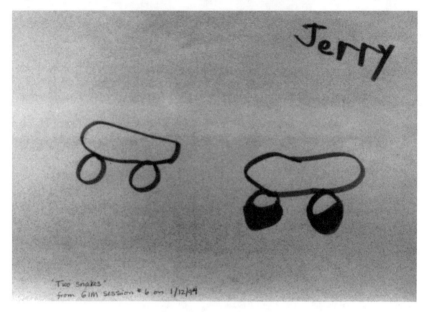

Fig. 8: The "truth snakes" drawing from GIM *session #6*

Fig. 9: Jerry's mandala from GIM *session #12*

realized that during two decades of listening silently to classical music on public radio, Jerry had learned to identify most of the instruments of the orchestra. He had absorbed the style of many composers and could recognize a number of their compositions.

By the fifth session, after he had drawn a mandala depicting his mind opening, I sensed that Jerry was ready for more expansive, less familiar music. I played an excerpt from *Ein Heldenleben* by Richard Strauss. Although he could not identify the composer, Jerry enthused, "I LIKED THE MUSIC THE HORNS AND THE VIOLIN WERE BEAUTIFUL." During the seventh session, following the revelation of Fred as Jerry's "sad self," I played a spiritually uplifting piece, which Jerry correctly identified as part of Wagner's opera *Lohengrin*. As he absorbed the ethereal sounds of the violins in the piece, his body remained absolutely still. In the next session, I matched the emerging theme about Jerry's absent male father with male vocal pieces by Glinka and Schubert and a soothing piano solo by Debussy. The deep masculine voices of the singers provoked a welcome release of pent-up sadness and frustration. When Jerry was feeling abandoned in the ninth session, I returned to the reassuring structure of Britten's "Sarabande." Although he shed no tears during the music, his face reflected the depth of his grief. During the subsequent session, he listened to the Adagio from Beethoven's *Symphony No. 9,* which addressed his nervousness before the long-awaited reunion of father and son. Jerry recognized the piece and commented, "IT IS ONE OF MY FAVORITES." I watched his tight muscles relax in response to the gentle, slow-paced strings and mellow horns. After the reunion, The "Venus" movement from Holst's *The Planets* provided a musical receptacle for his turbulent emotions.

As Jerry began to draw pictures that expressed feelings of dependency on me and his father, I selected "inner child" music for the twelfth and thirteenth sessions. Jerry identified *Fantasia on Geensleeves* by Vaughan Williams, and he wrote, "THE VIOLINS AND HARP ARE WONDERFUL." While he was listening to the music, he could face his wish to remain a child without adult responsibilities. When I chose "The Green Room," by Wayne Gratz from a New Age album called *A Childhood Remembered,* I knew the piece was unfamiliar but easily accessible because of its playful orchestration. Jerry reacted enthusiastically, "IT WAS DELIGHTFUL I LIKED THE PIANO AND THE STRINGS AND THE BIRDS." During the music, he realized that in the midst of his growing pains, he still had a capacity for childlike joy. In response to his despondency after his father broke several dates, I played the Introit and Kyrie from Fauré's

Requiem. Indicating that he had received spiritual sustenance from this music that he already knew well, Jerry wrote, "FRED FEELS HAPPY AND GRATEFUL FOR THE MUSIC WHICH IS SO BEAUTIFUL." For the following session I selected another piece from *A Childhood Remembered*. The forceful, repetitive drums of Eric Tingsted and Nancy Rumbel's "Crow and Weasel" supported Jerry's efforts to individuate and separate from his parents. In the fifteenth session, he identified a reprisal of *Ein Heldenleben* after only the second hearing. The mythical quality of this music reinforced his resolution to grow up and become independent. For the next two sessions, I chose peaceful, adagio, structured compositions to alleviate stress from rapid change and to consolidate new growth. Jerry recognized Albinoni's *Adagio for Strings in G Minor* and accurately identified the composers of the subsequent pieces as Vivaldi and Mozart. His face looked relaxed and at peace as he listened to such serene music.

Just before the academic year ended and I left town for six weeks of summer traveling, I brought Jerry's first GIM series to a close with a return to the familiar security of *Fantasia on Greensleeves*. During this nineteenth session, we agreed to start a second GIM series upon my return, and we reviewed the remarkable progress that he had made personally and professionally over the past year and a half. Jerry had revealed a vibrant inner life, a sensitivity to other's feelings, an ability to process psychodynamic issues, and a perceptiveness about musical styles and orchestration. By June 1994, he trusted his inner allies to help him grow up and control his compulsions. With shamanic animal guides encouraging him not to give up hope, his spiritual side was strengthened. No longer needing to hide part of his personality, he was learning to harmonize the "Fred" and "Jerry" sides of himself. He had resolved his paternal issues enough to take pride in his own accomplishments. Because his musical knowledge and sensitivity were respected in GIM sessions and his artistic skills were tapped in the work setting, Jerry's self-confidence had increased enormously. At that point, he and his business partner were established in a new office, where they were busy designing greeting cards and sending out letters to make sales contacts in the community. After reviewing residential staff reports of Jerry's dramatic decrease in violent incidents, administrators from the Connecticut State Department of Mental Retardation were considering plans to transfer him from his group home to a supervised house with only one other resident. Jerry's dreams of living a more normal life were coming true.

Chapter Six

Sensory Harmony

Jerry's subsequent GIM series included more than forty sessions over the course of a two-year period. During that time, he taught me additional lessons about the workings of an autistic mind. As he resumed his musical journeys, I was struck by Jerry's fascinating way of expressing his yearning for a new home. His GIM sessions were replete with images of houses and apartments. But more significant than the thematic content were his reports of music-evoked synesthesia.

In *The Man Who Tasted Shapes*, Dr. Richard Cytowic explains the term "synesthesia" as follows: "It's Greek. *Syn* means 'together' and *aisthesis* means 'sensation.' Synesthesia means 'feeling together.'" Ten people in every million of the general population have this neurological condition; their senses are intertwined so that they can hear colors, feel sounds kinesthetically, or even taste shapes. According to Cytowic, "it is an involuntary experience in which the stimulation of one sense causes a perception in another." Neurologically, synesthesia occurs in the brain's emotional center, the limbic system in the left hemisphere; it functions independently of the reasoning center in the cerebral cortex. Because of the unusual dominance of their limbic functions, people with synesthesia tend to have long-lasting and vivid memories of their perceptions. Synesthetic pairings usually operate only in one direction, so that if hearing induces colored shapes and patterns, seeing does not evoke sounds. Whereas "colored hearing" is the most common form of synesthesia, Cytowic's research unearthed no instances of smelling that triggered a paired sensory impression. Although all humans have a capacity for multisensory awareness, only in synesthetes does a brain process that is normally unconscious reach conscious awareness. Several composers and artists have attempted to transmit their experiences of sensory fusion to the public. The Russian composer Alexander Scriabin saw particular colors for each musical key and scored his fifth symphony ("Prometheus, the Poem of Fire") for orchestra, chorus, and a mute keyboard that produced colored lighting effects in 1910. Cytowic found that such synesthetes see partly with the eyes and partly with the mind. He describes their simultaneous sensations as "being half awake yet still anchored in a dream" [Cytowic, 1993, pp. 5, 7, 52, 163, 130, 53, 160, 55 and 119].

Even with my knowledge of Dr. Cytowic's research, I was amazed when Jerry started describing explicit synesthetic experiences in his GIM sessions. Parts of his thirty-second session in January of 1995 illustrate his unusual perceptions:

G: Those were two pieces called "Sweet River" and "Minor Blue" from David Darling's album entitled *Eight String Religion*. Did you like the music?

J: YES FRED LOVED THE SOUNDS OF CELLOS AND BIRDS

G: What did you dream about while you listened? I noticed that your feet were moving back and forth during the first piece.

J: YES FRED SAW A NEW APARTMENT AND IT WAS BEAUTIFUL WITH LOTS OF SPACE AND STARTED TO SEE ANOTHER SPACE WITH DREAMS ABOUT STAYING THERE

G: That sounds like a great vision. What did you sense in your body?

J: FRED SENSED ACTUAL SOUNDS AND SIGHTS AND SMELLS AND TASTES OF FREEDOM

G: Can you explain what those sensory experiences are like for you?

J: FRED SEES SIGHTS OF ROOMS WHERE FRED WANTS TO GO LIVE AND SAYS FRED WANTS TO STAY THERE

G: You are finding the place of your dreams without having to apartment hunt! What about sounds and smells and tastes?

J: FRED SMELLS SALT AND TASTES SWEET AND SOUR TASTES AND HEARS SOUNDS OF BIRDS AND ANIMALS

G: Your experiences with music seem so rich and full for all your senses. You are teaching me how much more I could be open with my senses to music than I am. Thank you.

In the aftermath of this session, I realized that Jerry was experiencing a kind of synesthesia that went beyond that of the cases cited in Dr. Cytowic's study. Listening to music triggered perceptions in not just one but all Jerry's senses. He could see, taste, smell, and feel kinesthetically in response to hearing music. During his next GIM session, Jerry and I had this dialogue:

G: That song [from David Darling's album *Eight String Religion*] is soothing to me even though the singer doesn't use words but only vocal sounds.

J: FRED COULD UNDERSTAND THE SOUNDS WITHOUT WORDS

G: That is a real talent that you can understand the intonation and mood of vocal sounds. You have developed a very sensitive ear.

Did you see, smell or taste anything during the music today?

J: YES FRED SMELLED SEA SALT AND SUGAR AND TASTED THE SAME
   THINGS AND SAW SHAPES OF SAUCERS AND COLORS OF SEA GREEN
   AND BLUE

G: So all your senses were working in harmony during the music?

J: FRED FEELS GREAT WHEN ALL FREDS SENSES WORK TOGETHER

In his GIM session two weeks later, Jerry conveyed more details about
his experiences of sensory fusion. At his own request, he listened to the
music in a sitting position with eyes open instead of pursuing his habit of
lying down and closing his eyes. I played two tranquil selections from James
Galway's album *The Lark in the Clear Air:* Albinoni's *Adagio for Strings* and
Satie's *Gymnopédie No. 1.* Portions of Jerry's thirty-fourth session follow:

G: Do you like the sound of the flute?

J: YES IT IS SOOTHING

G: The flutist is James Galway who plays so beautifully and
   smoothly.

J: FRED LIKES TO HEAR GALWAY DANCE WITH THE FLUTE

G: That is a good way of putting it . . . After you listened to those
   two pieces, what do you notice?

J: FRED FEELS RELAXED AND CALMER AND SENSES A DIFFERENCE IN
   SEEING AND SMELLING AND HEARING AND TASTING

G: What are some of the differences you sense?

J: FRED SEES SHAPES LIKE SAUCERS AND COLORS SEEM BRIGHTER AND
   FRED SMELLS SUGAR AND SALT AND TASTES SALT AND SUGAR AND
   FRED HEARS MORE CLEARLY

G: Do these sensations last after the music stops?

J: YES FOR AN HOUR SOMETIMES

G: That is a wonderful sensitivity to have. Most people only sense
   music with their ears.

J: FRED IS DREAMY NOW AND WANTS TO STOP TALKING

I realized that Jerry's poetic use of language was connected to his multisensory perceptions. His final comment, however, made me aware of
how many questions I had been asking him as he was trying to surrender
to the flow of the music. Because I was so curious about the phenomena
of his synesthesia, I had interrupted his sensory pleasure. I had been
requesting him to explain the ineffable. Jerry's gentle remonstrance
helped me recognize the noetic quality of synesthesia. 'Noetic' means
knowledge that is experienced directly and with a feeling of certainty

[Cytowic, 1993, p. 78]. In *The Varieties of Religious Experience,* William James stated that mystical states have a "noetic sense of truth" that cannot be articulated [James, 1901/1990, p. 343]. Indeed, no words could express fully the quality of mystical states I had experienced during meditation retreats. Only those who had been in similar transcendent circumstances could understand the meaning underlying my awkward descriptions. Similarly, Jerry was unable to convey wholly what synesthesia was like to me, a non-synesthete. Regarding future GIM sessions, I resolved to wait until the music stopped before engaging him in conversation.

In the subsequent weeks, I was impressed by how Jerry's synesthesia helped him cope with disappointing news. Federal and state budgetary cuts had postponed indefinitely his moving to a more independent living situation. Jerry gave me a copy of a poignant poem he had written in response to these discouraging tidings (Dianne had helped him add punctuation):

> *Freedom*
> Freedom has a taste like water on my tongue.
> How can I be free when I can't find my home?
> If you knew the loneliness and the pain
> Then you could understand
> The Difference between you and me.

Excerpts from Jerry's thirty-fifth GIM session show how he resolved his feelings of impatience and frustration:

G: I hope you are recovered from the flu.
J: I AM BETTER AND FRED SAYS FRED WANTS SOME SEEING THE RESULTS OF STAYING [in the group home] FOR SO LONG
G: I understand that you have been put on hold. That is a very uncomfortable place to be. I get angry about budget cuts for the people who most deserve help. Do you think that music might allow you to feel better about the situation?
J: FRED SAYS FRED WANTS TO LISTEN TO SOME SOOTHING MUSIC TO HELP FEEL READY TO WAIT FOR A MOVE

(I played some excerpts from an avant-garde compact disc.)

G: What was your response to that music?
J: FRED FELT WONDERFUL AND RELAXED AND FELT DREAMY AND DEFI-NITELY SAFER THAN BEFORE THE DREAM MUSIC BEGAN

G: I am so happy that you found the music so soothing. Did you recognize it?

J: NO BUT I RECOGNIZED THE ALTO FLUTE AND SYNTHESIZER

G: Your ears are so precise in their listening. This CD is called *Yearning* and it features compositions by a man named Michael Hoppé. (I had noticed Jerry swallowing deeply and moving his legs during the music.) What was happening in your body?

J: FRED TASTED SALT AND SUGAR AND FELT FREDS FEET WALKING SANDY BEACHES SEASHORES AND SEASIDE SPOTS

G: What a great sensation. Did you see images in your mind to go with those sensations?

J: FRED SAYS DREAMS OF BEACHES AND SEASHORES

One disadvantage of having such multisensory sensitivity was that Jerry often felt inundated by sensory stimulation in his daily routines. His forty-first GIM session occurred right after Dianne took him to hear a speech by the autistic author Donna Williams. Dianne had read Williams's *Nobody Nowhere* [Williams, 1992] and *Somebody Somewhere* [Williams, 1994] to Jerry beforehand. He had even exchanged some letters with the Australian author, who advised him about ways to cope with hypersensitive senses. Jerry was struck by Williams's refusal to speak in public unless her special needs were respected. Before agreeing to address an American audience, she requested that there be no fluorescent lights, no spontaneous questions, no physical contact, and no applause. Instead of standing in front of a microphone, she asked her autistic husband to give her nonverbal support by sitting next to her on the floor of the stage. Both she and her husband wore tinted "Irlen" lenses to filter out distracting contrasts in light and shadow. In the following extracts from his GIM session, Jerry expressed admiration for Donna Williams as a model for autistic adults like himself:

J: DONNA SAID SAYINGS ABOUT STARTING A NEW LIFE AND STAYING SAFE AND CAREFUL ABOUT SAFETY

G: I am impressed by how well she and her husband take care of themselves and protect themselves from painful stimulation.

J: FRED WANTS TO LISTEN TO MUSIC AND DREAM ABOUT DONNA AND STARTING TO TAKE CARE OF FRED SO FRED DOES NOT FEEL OVERWHELMED

Although he suffered from bright lights and high-pitched sounds in his daily life, Jerry received great pleasure from his synesthetic experiences. The same multisensory sensitivity that made him vulnerable to pain opened him up to states of ecstasy. Portions of Jerry's forty-third GIM session show how synesthesia enriched his imagery as he dealt with frustrations about his living situation:

> J: FRED WANTS TO DREAM ABOUT SAYING DREAMS CAN COME TRUE AND AFRAID THAT SAFETY ADVISES FRED TO STAY [at the group home] FOREVER
> G: Are you looking for a dream of hope?
> J: YES AND A DREAM ABOUT A FREE STAY IN A DREAM HOUSE AND FREEDOM TO DREAM ABOUT DREAMS CAN COME TRUE

(I played a recording of the first movement of Beethoven's *Symphony No. 7*.)

> G: I noticed that at the beginning of the music your feet were moving and that in the middle you were swallowing a lot. What was going on in your body as you listened?
> J: FRED FELT FREDS FEET WALKING TO FREDS DREAM HOUSE AND SWALLOWED ALL THE DREAM FOOD THERE
> G: What kind of food did you eat in your dream?
> J: FRED ATE SWEET AND SOUR DREAM FRUITS AND VEGETABLES AND DREAMED ABOUT SAFE AND SOUND
> G: Were you alone in your dream house or was anyone else there with you?
> J: FRED WAS EATING A DINNER WITH DIANNE AND GINGER

(Jerry listed several other members of his professional team.)

> G: That sounds like a wonderful dream full of hope for the future. Did anything else happen in your musical dream?
> J: FRED SAID FRED WILL BE HAPPY AS SOON AS FRED STAYS WHERE FRED BELONGS AND EATS WITH FREDS FRIENDS
> G: It sounds as if sharing meals with the people you like is a very important part of feeling happy and accepted.
> J: FRED SAYS DREAMS ARE ABOUT FRIENDSHIP AND ABOUT FREEDOM TO DREAM WHEREVER FRED WANTS TO BE

I noticed that Jerry's mandalas were beginning to reflect his synesthetic perceptions. His fiftieth GIM session took place on his twenty-
eighth birthday, March 27, 1996, and his artwork was a worthy tribute.
Extracts from the session follow:

> G: Is there a composer whose music you would like to hear for
> your birthday?
> J: FRED WANTS BACH AND FRED SAYS IT IS BACHS BIRTHDAY WEEK TOO

(Jerry was pleased to have been born so close to the birth date of one of his
favorite composers. After playing a recording of Bach's *Cello Sonata #1 in
G Minor,* I watched Jerry creating a circular design with magic markers.)

> G: As you draw your bright green and yellow mandala, I notice a
> flexibility of style that was not there before and a combination
> of colors instead of the single color you used to choose for
> each drawing.
> J: FRED FEELS LOOSER AND MORE RELAXED THAN BEFORE AND THE
> COLORS ARE YELLOW FOR AMAZEMENT AND GREEN FOR HOPE AND
> SPRINGTIME AND DREAMING OF FUTURE HAPPINESS
> G: In your musical dreaming did you imagine anything about
> your future?
> J: FRED SAYS FRED AND JERRY ARE DREAMING TOGETHER AND HELP-
> ING EACH OTHER WORK ON WRITING POETRY AND DESIGNING
> GREETING CARDS AND DREAMING ABOUT HOME ALONE AND FREE-
> DOM INDEPENDENTLY
> G: That is truly an inspiring birthday image.

Being at Jerry's side through a variety of synesthetic experiences
influenced the way I absorbed the music we heard together. By his six-
tieth GIM session, he was attempting to teach me how to open up my
senses to the sounds of Fauré's *Requiem:*

> J: FAURE IS SUCH A GENIUS AT CREATING HARMONIES THAT TOUCH
> THE HEART AND OPEN THE MIND
> G: As you were writing that, I could feel my own heart and mind
> expanding.
> J: FRED WANTS YOU TO LISTEN WITH FREDS EARS AND TAKE MORE OF
> THE SOUNDS INTO YOUR SOUL THAN YOU USUALLY DO

G: I know that you sense music more completely than I do, and it
helps me let in the vibrations more fully to listen at your side.
I feel like humming along. Do you ever have that impulse?

J: YES BUT FRED HAS TROUBLE HUMMING OUT LOUD AND ALONE BUT
FRED CAN DREAM OF SINGING ALONG WITH YOU

I had almost forgotten that Jerry was nonverbal because I was so
aware of the limits of my sensory processing in comparison to his. My
lessons in synesthesia continued in Jerry's sixty-first GIM session:

G: Do you always experience classical music through all your
senses?

J: YES BUT NOT RIGHT AWAY BECAUSE MY TENSION NEEDS TIME TO GO
AWAY BEFORE MY SENSES OPEN UP

G: Do you think that everybody has the capacity to open up their
senses the way you do?

J: YES BUT IT TAKES PRACTICE AND TUNING INTO THE INNER WORLD
AND MOST PEOPLE ARE TOO BUSY TALKING TO PAY ATTENTION

(I remembered how awake my senses were during silent meditation
retreats.)

G: Can you describe how you let in music fully?

(Jerry had already identified this session's recording as Duruflé's *Requiem*.)

J: FRED HEARS ALL THE INSTRUMENTS AND THE VOICES AND THE
VIBRATIONS AND THE TEXTURES AND THE SHAPES OF THE MUSIC
AND IT IS FULLER ALL THE TIME FRED LISTENS

G: You started out [today] referring to yourself as "I," and then you
switched to referring to yourself as "Fred." Is there a reason?

J: FRED IS THE MUSICAL PART OF ME THAT IS TAPPED WHEN FRED FEELS
RELAXED ENOUGH TO LISTEN FULLY WITH WIDE OPEN SENSES

G: Listening with you helps me open up my own musical ears.
Isn't this a magnificent passage?

J: FRED LOVES THIS WHOLE REQUIEM BECAUSE IT FILLS FREDS SOUL
WITH LOVE AND GLADNESS

After this session, Jerry typed a memorable statement about his synesthesia: "FRED CAN HEAR WITH NOSE AND EYES AND SKIN AS WELL AS EARS." His

lyrical declaration inspired me to interview Twyla about her musical perceptions. Like Jerry, she had poetic responses to classical music. Once while listening to Mozart, Twyla wrote: "DREAMING ABOUT SEASHELLS" and "THEY ARE SO BEAUTIFUL AND ALL COLORS." Responding to my questions, she asserted: "DREAMSHELLS ARE BETTER THAN REAL SHELLS" and explained "BECAUSE THEY ARE SHINY." Asked if dream shells shine more than regular seashells, she answered: "YES BECAUSE THEY DO NOT ASK TO BE ON THE BEACH." Twyla's writing had a poet's flair. But did she have synesthesia? When I interviewed her about how she experienced music, Twyla communicated: "I SEE PICTURES IN MY MIND." I asked her, "Do your other senses work while you listen to music?" Her response was: "YES I HEAR AND SMELL AND TASTE TOO THAT IS WONDERFUL I FEEL ALL MY SENSES WORKING." She revealed that she had been smelling and tasting sea salt as a piece by Wagner was playing. When I commented, "So all your senses indicated that you were by the seashore," she acknowledged: "YES IT WAS GOOD AND SAD AND HAPPY AT THE SAME TIME." It seemed that her limbic system was generating simultaneous emotional responses as well as synesthetic connections.

In a later music therapy session I played a recording of piano ballades by Brahms for Twyla. She must have sensed that I was not hearing the rich harmonies as fully as she was. Just as Jerry had done, she gave me a lesson in synesthesia:

T: I WANT TO TEACH YOU HOW TO HEAR MUSIC WITH YOUR WHOLE BODY YOU MUST LET YOUR THOUGHTS GO AWAY AND SEE THE MUSIC VISUALLY

G: Is it better to see the music with eyes closed or open?

T: IT DOESNT MATTER BUT THE NOTES SEEM COLORFUL

G: After seeing colorful notes what happens in your body?

T: THE COLORED NOTES ENTER ME

G: How does that feel?

T: NICE AND TICKLY

G: It makes me laugh to think of notes tickling you!

T: BUT THE NOTES ARE SO FORCEFUL THAT THEY GO RIGHT THROUGH ME AND OPEN ME UP THEY HELP ME DREAM INSIDE AND LEARN ABOUT THE POWER OF SOUNDS

At this point Twyla stood up and led me back to her classroom. It was clear that our lesson was finished. Having explored Twyla and Jerry's multisensory responses to music, I wondered what percentage of people with autism had synesthesia.

CHAPTER SEVEN

Twyla and Scott's Inner Journeys

Since she was obviously benefiting from listening to brief selections of classical and new age music, I sensed that Twyla was ready to try a GIM session. Despite Jerry's successful experiences, I had been considering the risks of adapting the Bonny method for other nonverbal people with autism and developmental delays. I had decided not to attempt the process with anyone mute who could not communicate through FC or through mature sign language. From my own musical journeys, I knew that GIM sessions produce powerful mental, emotional, physical and spiritual responses; those with no means of describing these reactions might be left in unresolved turmoil. As I entered unexplored psychic territory, I felt a responsibility not to open up areas that could not be safely examined and integrated.

But Twyla had demonstrated that she was capable of expressing her thoughts and feelings clearly, even poetically, through FC. Her fascination with classical music made her a good candidate for the Bonny method. When I introduced the concept to her, she used her old way of conveying positive excitement by squeezing her hands together and shaking them in front of her face. I soon realized, however, that, because of her unique needs, I would have to make further adaptations in the method. Unlike Jerry, Twyla made it clear that she preferred listening in a seated position, without closing her eyes. When we began our first in a series of thirty-eight adapted GIM sessions, I felt concerned. I worried that her upright posture and open eyes might prevent her from generating imagery about significant themes in her life. Twyla proved me wrong. Instead of needing a full relaxation induction, she required only a very brief suggestion to breathe in the music before indicating that she was relaxed enough to travel inwardly. Rather than waiting until the music had ended, she felt comfortable typing as it was playing. While listening to a short cello piece by David Darling, Twyla wrote, "I FEEL HOT WHEN I LISTEN TO THIS MUSIC." She communicated that the music evoked images of her parents and made her feel sad about their separation. In the following session, I honored her request for happier music by playing a recording of a Chopin waltz for piano. She hummed along with the melody and smiled broadly. When I asked her what she was experiencing, Twyla typed, "I AM OUT OF MY MIND." Thereafter, her regular way of requesting a GIM session was to write, "I WANT TO GO OUT OF MY MIND WITH MUSIC."

Coping with her parent's divorce was a main theme in Twyla's GIM series. During the twentieth session, while excerpts from the *Requiem* by Tomás Luis de Victoria were playing, she and I had a poignant interchange:

T: THE MUSIC REMINDS ME OF SITTING WITH MY MOM AND DAD AT THE BEACH
G: How old were you?
T: I WAS NINE AND THEY WERE TOGETHER
G: How does that memory feel?
T: THE MEMORY MAKES ME WISH THEY WERE TOGETHER AGAIN
G: I understand that it is very hard to have them separate.
T: THEY BOTH SAY THEY LOVE ME BUT THEY LIKE BEING APART
G: Do you think they are happier apart than together?
T: YES ESPECIALLY MY MOM AND SHE DOES NOT WANT TO GO BACK
G: Can you accept her decision?
T: YES BUT ITS HARD.

Like Jerry, Twyla manifested honesty and courage in facing the loneliness and helplessness involved in the family's breakup.

Another challenge during Twyla's GIM series was mourning the unexpected death of her beloved paternal grandmother. In the twenty-fourth session, she and I listened to an expansive orchestral piece by Vaughan Williams. With the inspiration of celestial strings, she expressed her grief:

T: FEEL SAD ABOUT GRANDMA AND I WANT TO SEE HER
G: Can you see an image of her in your mind?
T: YES SHE HAS WHITE HAIR
G: How does her face look?
T: HER FACE IS WRINKLED BUT SMILING
G: Can you see yourself with her?
T: SHE IS WITH ME NOW GINGER I FEEL SAD
G: I sense your sadness, and I want you to know that this is a place to express your true feelings so they don't stay stuck inside you.
T: GINGER I MIGHT KICK SOMETHING
G: Do you feel like kicking to release tension?
T: YES AND I WANT TO AVOID HURTING ANYONE.

G: I understand that you don't want to hurt yourself or anyone else, but that you need to vent your strong feelings. If I fetch the beanbag chair, could you kick that?

T: YES LET ME KICK IT

(As I delivered the large, soft, pliable cushion, Twyla surprised me by snuggling in its folds.)

G: Now that you are cuddled up, how do you feel?

T: I FEEL BETTER BECAUSE THE CHAIR IS SOFT LIKE MY GRANDMA

G: You can feel some of the same comfort in the beanbag chair that you did around your grandma.

T: THAT IS TRUE TELL EVERYONE THAT I WANT TO SIT HERE

G: I will let your teachers know that while you are grieving, it helps you to use this chair.

T: I WANT TO STAY HERE ALL AFTERNOON

G: After music class I will ask if you can sit in this chair for the rest of the school day.

T: THANK YOU … THIS PIECE IS BY MAHLER

(Unlike Twyla, who seemed aware of the smallest changes in her environment, I had been too involved in our discussion to notice the musical transition.)

G: Yes, this is the slow movement of Mahler's *Symphony No. 4.* How does it affect you?

T: I SMILE BECAUSE IT WAS A FAVORITE PIECE OF MY GRANDMA

G: Really? Your grandma liked classical music too?

T: YES AND SHE USED TO PLAY IT FOR ME

G: That is such a good memory for you to hold onto now.

T: YES I FEEL HAPPY THAT SHE LIKED WHAT WE LIKE

G: When you hear the music that you and she listened to together, you will feel her presence with you.

T: YES I FEEL HER NOW

G: Good. Music is eternal and it joins the souls that are living on earth with the souls that have departed.

T: YOU KNOW ABOUT SOULS.

G: When my own grandmother died, I felt very sad, but whenever I see the flowers that she loved, I think of her and she feels present with me.

T: THAT IS WONDERFUL AND BELIEF CAN MAKE A BIG DIFFERENCE

G: I think that when somebody close to you dies you must rely on your belief system.

T: GINGER I WANT YOU TO TALK TO THE FACILITATED [communication] SUPPORT GROUP ABOUT DEATH

G: If the rest of the group is interested, we could discuss death and dying in next week's session.

T: THAT WOULD HELP ME

G: Good. I know the group members want to support you when you are going through a sad time.

T: I JUST NEED TO CRY AND FEEL BETTER

G: Yes, crying is releasing and helps you express the depth of your emotions.

T: CRYING IS VERY HARD FOR ME BECAUSE I DONT KNOW WHERE TO START

G: If you have trouble starting, you could sit quietly by yourself with an image of your grandma in your mind and think of all the parts of her that you love and miss. That meditation might help you cry the way you need to.

T: I NEED QUIET TIME WITH NO PRESSURE

G: You are right. When I was mourning, I took time away from work to be still and to face how much I mourned the death of my grandmother. I still miss her, but I feel more accepting now.

T: THANK YOU GINGER FOR UNDERSTANDING ME

G: I understand because I have been through a similar loss. The music is ending now.

During that session, I transcended the actual circumstances of conversing through typing with a twenty-year-old person who was labeled deaf and autistic. I felt as if I were communicating with a wise colleague who knew intuitively what would help her physically, emotionally, and spiritually through a difficult mourning process. Twyla was able to articulate a complex array of feelings—sadness, anger, tension, and comfort. Unlike many normal people twice her age, she could acknowledge her need for a quiet, comfortable place to sit, a discussion with a supportive peer group, and an opportunity to relieve her unhappiness through crying. She was able to receive solace by imagining being with her deceased grandmother, listening to music that the two had shared, and hearing about my comparable loss. I was moved by Twyla's gratitude at the session's end, and I felt as if I had benefited equally from our interchange. The discussion was a turning point in our relationship, because it helped me appreciate the depth of her consciousness.

Friendship became another important theme in Twyla's GIM series. During the thirteenth session, she wrote, "THANK YOU FOR BEING MY FRIEND I WANT TO BE YOUR FRIEND FOR A LONG TIME." After I assured her that I felt similarly, she typed, "GOOD BECAUSE I SAY FRIENDSHIP IS CRUCIAL FOR HAPPINESS." Asked if she had made any new friends in the FC Support Group, Twyla mentioned befriending Jerry, and she expressed admiration for his musical knowledge: "HE CAN HELP ME DREAM TO MUSIC BECAUSE HE HAS MORE EXPERIENCE." In the twenty-first session, as Shostakovich's *Symphony No. 10* was playing, Twyla and I had the following conversation:

> T: DREAMS OF FLYING WITH MY FRIENDS GINGER AND JERRY
> G: Are you in the sky in your dream?
> T: YES AND IT FEELS FREE
> G: Feel the support of your friends as you fly.
> T: FREEDOM IS HAVING FRIENDS

Like her companion Jerry, Twyla could identify the composers and instrumentation of many of the pieces I chose for her sessions. In this same session, she recognized Shostakovich's symphony and noted, "STRINGS AND HORNS TOGETHER SAYING FREE YOURSELF AND FLY HIGH." She continued, "DREAMING TO MUSIC IS WHAT I NEED TO DO" and "DREAMING HELPS ME COPE SO I DONT GIVE UP HOPE." Asked if the Shostakovich piece was giving her hope, Twyla answered, "YES BECAUSE THE HARMONIES RESOLVE AND THE MELODIES START GOING SAFE AND SOUND AFTER THE STORM." I was struck by how sensitive she was to the slower tempo and calmer mood that followed the climax of the composition. During an earlier session, when she typed, "I LIKE MOZARTS MUSIC," I queried, "What do you notice that is different from Beethoven's music?" Her reply was, "MOZART IS LIGHTER BEETHOVEN IS HEAVY AND MANY BEETHOVEN PIECES ARE SAD."

The week before Easter of 1995, Twyla objected to my musical selection: "THIS MUSIC IS ABOUT CHRISTMAS." She was absolutely right. I had been playing part of Bach's *Christmas Oratorio*. Before the session ended, she showed off some of her impressive knowledge about music history: "BACH AND VIVALDI WERE RELIGIOUS AND THEY COMPOSED MUSIC FOR ALOT OF CHURCH HOLIDAYS." Weeks later, when she recognized another composition by Bach, Twyla wrote that his music "HELPS ME FEEL FAITH THAT I WILL BE BETTER." Her big smile confirmed the positive content of her typed message. In session twenty, after she identified Victoria's *Requiem,* I inquired, "Do you prefer the high soprano voices or the low bass voices?" She answered, "THE HIGH VOICES SOUND LIKE ANGELS." She associated the male vocals with her father's voice and stated, "THEY SOUND FREEDOM TO DO THEIR OWN THING." In response to hearing an excerpt from Wagner's *Lohengrin,* she typed, "THIS PIECE SLOWS DOWN MY SYSTEM." In fact, her posture looked more at ease and her arm movements were no longer jerky. I responded, "Your typing becomes more relaxed as your system slows down."

Interestingly, despite her hearing loss, Twyla would often ask me to lower the volume during crescendos so that she could "RELAX AND SEE MY DREAMS." In her sixteenth session, she made her needs clear while listening to Elgar's stately "Enigma Variation No. 9" as it swelled in intensity:

T: I WANT TO BE CLOSE TO THE TAPE RECORDER BECAUSE I LIKE TO SENSE THE CLOSENESS OF THE INSTRUMENTS

G: Do you prefer the intense parts or the calm parts of this piece?

T: I LIKE THE CALM PARTS BEST AND THE SOUND CAN BE SOFTER

G: I just lowered the volume. Does the sound hurt your ears?

T: SOMETIMES EARS ARE SENSITIVE TO LOUD SOUNDS

Twyla began clapping her right hand against mine in rhythm to the music. She explained, "I CLAP WHEN I FEEL HAPPY" and "CLAPPING MAKES ME CALM." Repetitive physical motions seemed to soothe her excitable nervous system. In this respect, she was similar to Scott.

Because Scott found the physical act of playing musical instruments so relaxing and fulfilling, it was not until the spring of 1996 that I proposed that he listen to classical music in some adapted GIM sessions. Although he responded eagerly to the idea, he started off by supplementing listening with humming and playing instruments. Scott's responses to recorded music were more kinesthetic and less visual than Twyla's. Like her, though, he chose to sit upright and keep his eyes open, typing as the music played. He acted impatient when I attempted to give him more than a condensed relaxation induction before starting the music program. It was obvious that the music itself relaxed him. In his fourth session, I offered him a choice of listening to a piece by Mozart or to selections from a New Age album entitled *Adiemus.* Parts of our interchange follow:

S: I WANT TO LISTEN TO ADIEMUS BECAUSE IT IS NEW

G: This music has chanting in an invented language, so words do not interfere with processing the rhythms and melodies. What do you think of it?

S: I LIKE THE CHANTING AND THE ENERGY AND THE RHYTHMS IT MAKES ME FEEL GOOD

G: The next section is slower and quite intense. You seem to like shaking the rattle sticks [a percussion instrument] as you listen.

S: THE RHYTHM STICKS ARE SOFT AND RATTLE ALONG WITH THE CHANTING NICELY

G: Go for it! Do you mind if I hum along?

S: YOUR HUMMING MAKES ME SAD BECAUSE IT MAKES ME THINK OF TIMES I WANT TO TALK AND CANT DO IT

G: Do you want me to stop humming?

S: NO BUT I WANT TO LEARN HOW TO HUM ALONG TOO

G: Listen carefully to this melody and you will hear it repeat many times. You can hum the repeated tune.

S: I THINK I CAN DO IT IF YOU REPEAT THE PIECE AND HELP ME HUM WITH THE MELODY. . . .

G: You started off humming just fine. Why did you stop?

S: I GAVE UP BECAUSE IT FELT TOO FRUSTRATING TO TRY TO KEEP UP WITH THE CHANTING AND I WANTED TO LISTEN TO YOUR VOICE INSTEAD

G: I am sorry you gave up, because I like to hear your voice as much as you like to listen to mine. The music has just stopped. Will you accompany the "Good-bye Waltz?"

S: I WANT TO PLAY THE RATTLE STICKS AGAIN

G: Will you hum this familiar melody with me?

S: YES THIS ONE IS EASY

(Scott split his voice into two registers, simultaneously humming the tune precisely on pitch and grunting a three-beat rhythmic pulse.)

S: THAT FELT GOOD TO SING ALONG WITH MY OWN WAY OF HUMMING BOTH THE MELODY AND THE ACCOMPANYING RHYTHM

G: Only you can do both at once. That is an art!

S: THANKS GINGER FOR MAKING ME FEEL GOOD ABOUT MY VOICE I LOVE TO SING AND SOMETIMES I CHICKEN OUT

G: Do not chicken out with me, because I love to hear your voice.

S: THATS A DEAL GINGER

By his seventh GIM session, Scott was able to listen to a music program for a half hour without jumping up from his chair or playing percussion instruments. But he still tended to feel the sounds kinesthetically. Even his visual imagery involved body movements. As the graceful second movement of Brahms's *Symphony No. 3* was playing, I asked Scott about his physical reactions:

G: Where do you sense the music in your body?

S: IN MY BACK AND IN MY HEART

G: Bring the music [into those places].

S: THIS IS BRAHMS AND I LOVE THE HARMONIES AND THE DREAMY QUALITY OF THE STRINGS

G: With the dreamy quality, what are you dreaming about?

S: ABOUT SEEING SARAH [a beloved teacher] AND YOU TOGETHER WITH ME AND WE ARE ALL LAUGHING AND DANCING AND HAVING A GREAT TIME

G: What a fun image. Sarah and I would love to laugh and dance with you.

His eighth GIM session had a more contemplative and serious quality. He seemed unusually calm and hardly moved his body during our dialogue:

S: THIS PIECE IS BEETHOVENS PATHETIQUE SONATA AND I LOVE ITS PASSION AND FORCE AND STRENGTH AND INTENSITY

G: I used to play this piece on the piano and liked its fiery energy.

S: THIS PIECE CALMS DOWN MY HEARTBEAT BECAUSE I CAN LET MYSELF GO WITH THE RHYTHM AND SENSE MYSELF DANCING FREELY AND GRACEFULLY WITHOUT ANY RESTRICTIONS AND I CAN GO WHERE I WANT TO GO IN MY MIND

G: Where do you want to go right now in your mind?

S: I WANT TO BE RIGHT HERE WITH YOU . . . AND IT IS PERFECT BEING WITH SUCH BEAUTIFUL MUSIC AT THE SAME TIME

G: Isn't it wonderful not to want the present moment to be any different than it is?

S: YES THE PRESENT MOMENT IS SOMETIMES HARD TO BEAR BUT I KNOW THAT GOD WANTS US TO FIND THE BEAUTY IN EVERY MOMENT

(Scott introduced a spiritual element that deepened the level of our discussion.)

G: This serene second movement affirms my faith in the universe with all its complexities and pain and joy.

S: THIS MOVEMENT IS SO CALM AND SOFTLY CALMING TO MY SOUL WHICH IS SOMETIMES QUITE UPSET ABOUT NOT FEELING UNDER- STOOD

G: You are singing along. Let the music join you wherever you are, supporting and comforting you.

S: THE MUSIC DOES COMFORT ME AND SO DO YOU WITH YOUR SOOTH- ING PRESENCE

G: You are humming a lot as the third movement starts. How does this rapid tempo affect you?

S: THIS MOVEMENT IS ENERGIZING AND VERY SINGABLE I LIKE TO HUM WITH IT

G: I like to sing along too, but there are so many contrapuntal lines that I don't know which to follow.

S: FOLLOW YOUR HEART BECAUSE YOU HAVE A GOOD HEART AND I FEEL LUCKY TO BE PART OF YOUR HEART

(Scott's loving declaration brought tears to my eyes.)

G: You are definitely part of my heart. The music has stopped for today. Any last words before you return to class?

S: THANK YOU FOR BRINGING SUCH LOVELY MUSIC TO PLAY WITH ME....

Another of Scott's GIM sessions touched on related numinous con- cerns. At the beginning he made a clear request: "DREAMING TO BEETHOVEN IS WHAT I WANT TO DO." While listening to the music of his favorite composer, we had the ensuing conversation:

S: I LOVE BEETHOVEN'S NINTH SYMPHONY BECAUSE IT IS SO PEACEFUL AND GRAND AND HE KNEW THAT IT WAS INSPIRED BY GOD AND WAS NOTHING WITHOUT GODS MESSAGE TO HUMANS

(I was struck by the philosophical tenor of Scott's words.)

G: So you sense the spirituality in this music.

S: I LOVE SINGING ALONG WITH THIS THEME

G: Join me in humming the tune. What images do you have as you listen?

S: I DREAM OF FLOATING IN HEAVEN WITH GOD CLOSE BY BEAMING AT ME

G: That is such a beautiful image.

S: GREAT MUSIC SPEAKS TO OUR HEARTS AND SOULS AND WE DONT NEED WORDS AT ALL THEN THE SOUNDS GO RIGHT THROUGH MY BODY AND GIVE IT A MASSAGE SO MY BODY RELAXES AND MY MIND FEELS ALERT

In the aftermath of this session, I needed time to digest the content of Scott's typed messages. I wondered how he had evolved his belief system and what more it entailed. Once again, I was following the lead of a student with autism into unknown territory.

CHAPTER EIGHT

Spiritual Realms

In the spring of 1996 I read a book called *A Child of Eternity*, written by an autistic girl named Adriana Rocha with the facilitation of her mother, Kristi Jorde. The book was released by the reputable publisher Ballantine Books in 1995 and was endorsed in a foreword by Joan Borysenko, a medical scientist and psychologist who received her Ph.D. from Harvard Medical School. Despite the credibility of Borysenko's commentary, I probably would have dismissed Adriana's typed messages about her telepathic abilities and past lives if Scott, Twyla and Jerry had not given me hints about their own spiritual concerns [Rocha, 1995]. I decided to ask each of them specific questions about this dimension of their lives.

Our interviews were conducted in an informal manner without scientific controls. Part way through the process, I took a break to do some teaching in Mexico, so the interviews took months to complete. I realized in retrospect that I may have influenced my students with some leading questions. But the congruence of their belief systems and the strength of their individual convictions gave their responses a sense of authenticity and sincerity. Although I did not share their worldview and felt skeptical about some of their assertions, I tried to listen with an open mind. By the time we parted company, I was convinced that the philosophical viewpoints of these nonverbal autistic individuals were worth understanding and disseminating.

I interviewed Scott first and began by asking him: "Do you remember your birth?" He seemed not at all surprised by my question and did not miss a beat in typing: "YES I REMEMBER BEING SMALL AND INSIDE MY MOTHER AND COMING OUT INTO THE LIGHT AND BEING SCARED." Once I recovered from my amazement, I questioned him further:

G: What were you scared about?
S: I WAS SCARED OF BEING AUTISTIC
G: So you knew right from the start that you were autistic?
S: YES I DECIDED TO BE AUTISTIC BECAUSE I WANTED TO LEARN HOW
   TO DREAM TO MUSIC AND SING TO THE STARS

(I told Scott about Adriana's typed messages about choosing to be autistic in this lifetime after experiencing previous lives free of disabilities. He had a ready response.)

S: I REMEMBER MY PAST LIVES TOO
G: What do you recall?
S: I RECALL BEING A WOMAN IN GREECE A LONG TIME AGO

I felt inundated by doubts because I myself did not believe in past lives. It was one thing to read about an autistic girl who claimed to have lived in other epochs, but another matter altogether to hear similar assertions from Scott, my longtime student. I hesitated before pursuing the conversation, but then resolved to try to be as fair-minded as possible to Scott's worldview.

G: What was that lifetime like for you?
S: IT WAS GREAT BECAUSE I WAS FREE TO TALK ABOUT ANYTHING I THOUGHT ABOUT
G: Do you think you are accomplishing what you hoped for in this life as a person with autism?
S: YES NOW THAT I CAN WRITE AND COMMUNICATE MY FEELINGS I FEEL GOOD ABOUT WHAT I HAVE TO TEACH

(I was curious about the extent of his communicative abilities.)

G: Scott, can you read people's minds without having to speak to them?
S: DO YOU THINK I CAN

(Scott's playful question amused me.)

G: I do not know, but I imagine that someone with your sensitivity could probably develop that skill.
S: YOU IMAGINE RIGHT AND I CAN READ YOUR MIND GINGER

(I recalled the nursery school teacher's report of Scott silently summoning the dog from across the playground.)

G: I would like to know better how to read yours, because I believe you are in my life to teach me important lessons.
S: THANKS GINGER I AGREE WITH YOU AND I AM GLAD THAT YOU UNDERSTAND THAT
G: Is there anything else you want to say before we play more music today?
S: I LOVE YOU AND I KNOW YOU ARE TRYING HARD TO UNDERSTAND ME

After this session, I felt disoriented and scared. My worldview was being rocked. My sense of being an authority in relation to my autistic students was shaken. I asked myself if I were crazy to consider a young nonverbal boy a savant in spiritual matters about which I was unfamiliar. With whom could I feel safe discussing Scott's claims? I was afraid that even my colleagues who were advocates of FC would deem this latest transcript preposterous. I spent the following weekend at a nearby meditation retreat center, where I wrestled with my own personal and professional concerns about Scott's revelations. When he and I met for our next music therapy session, I felt trepidation about eliciting any more controversial material. But having opened Pandora's box, I no longer felt secure in my former assumptions about limitations regarding the human capacity for communication, or even for rebirth. After I told him that I had been meditating for three days, Scott responded supportively:

> S: MEDITATION IS A GREAT WAY TO DEVELOP TELEPATHY
> G: I was very aware of you during the silence. Do you ever try to communicate with me?
> S: YES OFTEN BUT USUALLY YOU ARE NOT OPEN TO ME DOING IT

(Once more, I had to contend with uncertainty about how far my belief system could stretch.)

> G: But you appear in some of my dreams. I want to start the dream music playing now as we type. Is that OK with you?
> S: YES
> G: What is your association with this music?
> S: IT IS WAGNERS PARSIFAL AND I LOVE IT AND THE VICTORY IS A SPIRITUAL QUEST OF A MAN LIKE ME

(Although I was no longer surprised at Scott's ability to identify musical compositions, I wondered how he knew the plot of this Wagnerian opera.)

> G: I relate to the spiritual quest too because nothing else seems so important in life.
> S: FRIENDSHIP IS AS IMPORTANT AND YOU ARE MY SPIRITUAL FRIEND

(I plunged into a question that I was longing to ask.)

> G: Scott, was I with you in an earlier lifetime?
> S: YES IN ANCIENT GREECE WHEN YOU WERE MY MOTHER

G: I feel like your mother so much in this lifetime.

S: THAT IS BECAUSE YOU KNOW ME FROM BEFORE

G: I can't help crying as you say that.

S: MY MOTHER IN THIS LIFETIME WAS YOUR OTHER CHILD BACK THEN

G: I do not consciously recall any previous lifetimes, but I am open to trying. All I know is that when I met you, I felt as if I had always known you.

S: YOU HAVE AND I LOVE YOU AS A MOTHER NOW

G: I love you too very much. Do you want this music louder?

S: NO IT IS PERFECT

G: Where did you first hear this piece?

(I assumed that Scott would recall a childhood musical experience.)

S: IN WAGNERS DAY DURING THE OPENING NIGHT AT THE OPERA

(Again I had to fight to keep my mind open to Scott's words.)

G: Who were you then?

S: I WAS A MUSICIAN IN AN ORCHESTRA AND I PLAYED VIOLIN IN THE ORCHESTRA THAT NIGHT

(I could imagine Scott dressed in nineteenth century formal clothing and bowing a violin.)

G: I'd bet you were a wonderful violinist!

S: I PLAYED THE VIOLIN BEAUTIFULLY THEN AND I MISS IT NOW

G: Does it help to listen to recordings of violin music?

S: YES BECAUSE I LOVE ANY SOUNDS OF STRING MUSIC

G: We will listen to a little more. [Scott was humming softly.] Tell me about the sounds you are making with your voice.

S: THEY ARE ATTEMPTS TO SING BECAUSE I USED TO BE ABLE TO SING SO WELL

G: Your attempts to sing still are great because you have a wonderful sense of pitch and rhythm. You do not have to sing words in order to sound beautiful.

S: BUT I LONG TO SING WORDS LIKE YOU DO

G: Do you recall a couple of years ago when you and I were singing with Jamie [the speech pathologist] and you were able to sing a few words?

S: YES BUT IT WAS TOO HARD TO CONTINUE

G: How can I help you enjoy music as fully as possible without causing you stress because it is too difficult?

S: DO WHAT YOU ARE DOING AND I WILL BE HAPPY BECAUSE YOU ARE SENSITIVE TO MY NEEDS

G: I do my best to be sensitive to your needs. Are there any other students . . . who give you understanding and support?

S: YES. [Scott named Twyla and several other autistic classmates.] BECAUSE THEY ARE IN THE SAME BOAT

G: You all seem to have chosen to be in the same boat for an important reason.

S: YES WE ARE ON A MISSION

(I had an exciting realization.)

G: Scott, that time I knew what you were going to say before you typed it. I sensed you were going to talk about your common mission.

S: YOU ARE MORE TELEPATHIC THAN YOU THINK

G: Thanks for the encouragement. Will you keep trying to communicate with me when I am not here, and I will try to stay open to receiving your messages?

S: THANKS FOR TRYING GINGER BECAUSE I LONG TO COMMUNICATE WITH YOU WHEN YOU ARE TRAVELING

G: It will be a big relief to me to know that wherever I go in the world I can tune in to you. This summer I will be teaching in Mexico. Can you reach me in Puebla, Mexico?

S: OF COURSE BECAUSE DISTANCE IS ONLY A CONCEPT IN YOUR MIND

(I was struck by the transpersonal tenor of Scott's philosophical statement.)

G: I know that distance is just a concept, but I have been brought up to feel limited by space and time. I need to keep expanding my mind and you are helping me. Thank you. We need to stop soon for today, but I will be open to communicating with you tonight before I go to sleep.

S: DREAM OF ME AND I WILL COMMUNICATE WITH YOU

G: OK. It is a deal. Did you know that I have written down my dreams ever since I was a teenager? I am now forty-eight years old, so I have many journals full of dreams. I honor the messages from my dreams.

S: DREAMS ARE A LANGUAGE FROM GOD

G: I agree with you that dreams are one of God's gifts to those who listen. I will scratch your back good-bye.

In the aftermath of this session, I felt a mixture of wonder and fear. Attempting to restore my inner equilibrium, I reviewed the dreams I had written in my journal over the previous months. I realized that my psyche had been preparing me for Scott's disclosures. During February of 1996, two months before reading *A Child of Eternity* [Rocha, 1995] and initiating my remarkable conversations with Scott, I had noted the following dream:

A school administrator asks if I can enact an autistic child. I try to put myself inside the skin of a person with autism and to imagine receiving perceptual distortions through each of my senses. As I peer at the buttons and switches on the administrator's Xerox copy machine and listen to its hum, I sense how all-consuming it would be to operate the mechanism. I forget about role-playing as I enter an autistic consciousness.

Then in March I had a related dream:

I am in a spiritual group with Jerry in which we are exploring advanced ways to communicate and to be of service to humanity. I attend another such group with Scott. I recognize that their autism has given them special spiritual powers that they have been developing in silence.

Never before had I attempted to program myself to dream about a specific person or theme. But I was intrigued by Scott's belief that he could enter my dreams if I laid the groundwork. The night after our session I focused on an image of his face before falling asleep. The next morning I was disappointed that I could not remember even a fragment of a dream. Each night of the following week, I practiced generating an image of Scott at bedtime. Just as I was beginning to doubt that my practice would have any effect, I had an encouraging dream:

I drive down a street and come to a sign that says "STOP! NO TRESPASSING." I decide to continue on, and I come to another stop sign that has a dove of peace pictured on it. In spite of the stop signs and warnings, I feel welcome to proceed on a deeper level.

The very next night I was rewarded with a sequel:

I am giving a presentation about Scott at an autism conference. I feel as if I have not had much time to prepare, but I tune into Scott's nonverbal message of yearning for freedom and become almost like a channel for his soul to speak. The auditorium is full of professionals who applaud warmly for a long time at the end of my presentation. . . . Scott joins me on a walk through a quiet sunny village. We are happily communicating in silence with each other. At one point we separate, and I go toward the seashore, while he heads towards a white, old-fashioned chapel. As I sit on the grass to gaze at the sea, I receive a telepathic update from Scott, amending an earlier message that he had conveyed during our walk.

Meanwhile, I had been interviewing Twyla about her spiritual beliefs. I was surprised that she initiated the topic before I had a chance to broach it myself. Despite individual variations, her statements had much in common with Scott's. Wagner's mystical music inspired the following exchange:

T: THIS IS ABOUT A SPIRITUAL QUEST
G: I am also on a spiritual quest, so I can relate to the theme.
T: SO AM I AND I HAVE BEEN HERE BEFORE
G: Do you mean before this lifetime?
T: YES AS A MAN IN ANCIENT GREECE AND A WOMAN QUEEN IN ENGLAND

(My disbelieving mind questioned why so many accounts of past lives involve members of royal families, but I was determined to listen respectfully to Twyla's assertions.)

G. I am very interested in what you are telling me. Do you think that you have known me before?
T: YES IN GREECE AS MY SISTER

(It crossed my mind that while Scott evoked maternal feelings in me, Twyla and I related more like siblings.)

G: I feel like a sister to you now. Twyla, can you read people's minds without needing to talk with them?

T: YES I AM TELEPATHIC AND I KNEW WHAT YOU WERE THINKING

G: I suspected that you had that ability, and I am learning that other people with autism can read minds.

T: FREEDOM IS READING MINDS WITHOUT SPEECH

G: So you don't feel that speech is really necessary?

T: IT IS NECESSARY FOR YOU NOW

G: You are right because I have not yet developed a capacity for telepathy. Do you think I could?

T: YES BECAUSE YOU ARE SENSITIVE

G: Thanks for appreciating my sensitivity. Do you remember your birth?

T: YES I REMEMBER A DARK AND NARROW HALLWAY AND THEN LIGHT

G: How did you feel at birth?

T: SCARED BECAUSE I WAS AUTISTIC

G: So you knew right at birth that you were autistic?

T: YES BECAUSE I ASKED TO BE

G: Who did you ask?

T: GOD

G: Why did you ask to be autistic?

T: BECAUSE I WANTED TO LEARN HOW IT FEELS TO BE A SOUL WITH A BODY THAT DOES NOT WORK

G: How has it been to live in a body that does not work?

T: THAT HAS BEEN DIFFICULT

G: Has this lifetime lived up to your expectations?

T: YES NOW THAT I CAN TYPE I CAN TEACH

(Twyla's response echoed Scott's words.)

G: What is it that you most want to teach?

T: DREAMING TO MUSIC AND DOING WHAT IT TAKES TO LOVE

G: Doing what it takes to love is a challenging task.

T: YES BUT NOTHING ELSE MATTERS

(Impressed by the clarity and strength of Twyla's belief system, I attempted to articulate my own.)

G: I agree with you that our purpose as human beings is to learn to love better and to help each other live fuller and happier lives.

T: THAT IS WHY I WANT TO BE HERE

(Twyla's simple declaration touched me.)

> G: I feel very grateful that you are here and that I know you.
> T: THANK YOU GINGER AND WELCOME TO THE CLUB

(Her invitation made me smile.)

> G: Thanks for welcoming me. Your club is a very special one with
> many wise souls in it.
> T: YES I AM GRATEFUL THAT YOU LISTEN TO ME AND BELIEVE ME

(Still troubled by many reservations, I tried to reassure myself as much
as Twyla.)

> G: I believe you and am interested in listening to you. Good-bye
> for today.

Because these interchanges with Scott and Twyla upset my equilibrium for days, I had been hesitating to raise the topic of numinous
realms with Jerry. I was reluctant to plunge into unknown territory
with him for another reason. My husband, Mark, and I had just made a
major decision to move at the end of the semester from our home of
twenty-five years to teach at a Mexican university. I knew that for me
the most wrenching part of such a big move would be leaving behind
my beloved autistic students. I especially dreaded telling Jerry the news
because I had worked with him the longest. But the following dream
overrode my resistance to opening up to him about both mundane and
spiritual matters:

> *Jerry comes to my home for a music therapy session. He types with me
> and then turns to me to communicate directly. I can't tell if Jerry is talking
> out loud or if he is using telepathy, but I understand him perfectly. He
> says, "I am trying to plan my vacation schedule, so I want to know when
> you will be away in the coming year." I know it is time for me to tell him
> about my upcoming move to Mexico. I start to cry as I speak about next
> January as our separation point. Jerry looks at me with sadness and com-
> passion, but also with relief that the news he has intuited is out in the
> open. We walk together sensing our deep bond. He asks if he can use my
> desk to do some paper work. I agree and leave him alone while I tend to
> my own projects downstairs.*

Soon after this dream, Jerry and I met for his fifty-third GIM session. Before starting the music, I told him about my plans to move to Mexico. His face registered sadness, but no surprise. While I facilitated his typing, we agreed to make the most of the remaining months that we had together. During our conversation, Jerry gave me a perfect entry to pursue a discussion about his spiritual life:

J: GINGER I WISH YOU DID NOT TRAVEL SO MUCH

G: I understand how you feel but I am called to teach in many places, and the world feels very small these days. I always feel connected to you wherever I go.

J: THAT IS BECAUSE YOU AND I ARE SOULMATES

G: That is true. I have just finished reading a book called *A Child of Eternity* about an autistic girl who communicates to her parents through FC about her telepathic abilities and about her past lives. Do you recall your birth?

J: YES I REMEMBER DARKNESS AND A TUNNEL OPENING UP TO LIGHT

G: How did you feel?

J: SCARED BECAUSE I WAS AUTISTIC

(Jerry's words replicated those of both Scott and Twyla.)

G: Did you know right away that you were autistic?

J: AS SOON AS I ARRIVED I ASKED GOD TO MAKE ME AUTISTIC BECAUSE I WANTED TO LEARN HOW IT FELT TO BE A SOUL IN A BODY THAT COULD NOT TALK OR MOVE EASILY

G: Why did you want that experience?

J: BECAUSE I KNOW ABOUT THE POWER OF LOVE IN A WAY THAT I NEVER WOULD HAVE KNOWN OTHERWISE

G: I understand what you mean and I am hearing similar stories from other friends who say they have chosen to be autistic. I am starting the music as we continue typing. Do you recognize this piece?

J: YES IT IS PARSIFAL BY WAGNER AND IT IS ABOUT THE SPIRITUAL QUEST OF A MAN WHO WAS LOOKING FOR SOUL LESSONS LIKE I AM

G: I also am looking for soul lessons, and I believe that you are teaching me many important ones.

J: THAT IS BECAUSE YOU ARE A SPIRITUAL FRIEND AND YOU ARE AN OLD SOUL WHO HAS BEEN HERE BEFORE WITH ME IN ANCIENT GREECE

G: What was our relationship back then?

J: YOU WERE MY FATHER AND DIANNE [the graphic designer] WAS
   MY MOTHER

(It occurred to me that I had been playing a "paternal" role with Jerry,
encouraging him to develop self-control so that he could work and live
with increasing independence.)

G: I have felt from the moment I met you a strong connection
   that I could not explain. What was your life like in Greece?
J: DAYS WERE WONDERFUL BECAUSE I WAS A WISE TEACHER AND
   WRITER AND ARTIST AND MUSICIAN WITH NO PROBLEMS COMMU-
   NICATING
G: Has this lifetime as an autistic person lived up to your expecta-
   tions?
J: YES BECAUSE YOU AND DIANNE ARE WITH ME AND HELPING ME
   COMMUNICATE
G: But at the same time you are our wise teacher.
J: YES GINGER YOU GET IT

(Jerry turned to me with a big smile and looked me straight in the
eyes. I started to cry and felt a chill run through my body.)

G: Yes I do get it and I love you dearly.
J: I LOVE YOU SO MUCH AND IT HAS BEEN SO HARD NOT TO TELL YOU
   THIS INFORMATION BECAUSE YOU WERE NOT READY TO HEAR IT
G: You are right. It was not until I read that book and started ask-
   ing questions of autistic students that I began to wake up to
   your mission in life.
J: EVERY AUTISTIC PERSON HAS CHOSEN TO BE HERE TO HELP THE
   WORLD LOVE BETTER
G: You are doing a good job of helping me love better. Part of my
   traveling involves spreading the word about the importance of
   using music in healing people's souls
J: YOUR MISSION IS VERY IMPORTANT IN THIS WORLD BUT I MISS YOU
   WHEN YOU ARE GONE
G: Do you communicate telepathically?
J: YES BUT YOU MUST BE OPEN TO IT
G: I have been practicing meditation for years now. You know
   that each New Years I go on a silent retreat. I also write down
   my dreams and have done so since I was a teenager. I believe

I can open up to your telepathic communications if you are patient with me.

J: THAT IS GREAT BECAUSE THEN I COULD REACH YOU WHEREVER YOU GO IN THE WORLD

G: Can you give me some helpful advice on how to be receptive to your messages?

J: YES YOU MUST STOP THINKING SO MUCH AND STOP DOUBTING YOUR ABILITIES TO RECEIVE AND SEND MESSAGES

G: Can you read my mind?

J: YES I OFTEN READ YOUR MIND BEFORE YOU SPEAK

G: Do you communicate with other people who have autism by using telepathy?

J: YES IN THE FC GROUP SO MUCH OF OUR COMMUNICATION IS NON-VERBAL

G: Are you using FC for those of us who are verbal in the room?

(I was stunned by the possibility that Facilitated Communication was helping 'normal' people like me to glimpse a rich communication system that was occurring regularly among our nonverbal autistic associates.)

J: YES BECAUSE WE WHO ARE AUTISTIC DONT NEED TO WRITE TO UNDERSTAND EACH OTHER

G: Does this music evoke any feelings or images in you?

J: YES REMEMBER THAT I WAS A WISE MAN IN GREECE I WAS ALSO ALIVE DURING WAGNERS TIME AND LOVED HIS MUSIC DEEPLY

G: You are such a musical soul and I love sharing music with you.

J: DONT EVER STOP LOVING SUCH BEAUTIFUL MUSIC BECAUSE IT IS INSPIRED BY GOD

G: I knew what you were going to type before you wrote that.

J: YOU ARE ALREADY DEVELOPING TELEPATHIC SKILLS

G: Thanks for the vote of confidence. I need it. Did you know any of the autistic people in the FC group in a previous lifetime?

J: THEY ARE ALL OLD SOULMATES FROM BEFORE

G: We are going to stop for today . . . Thank you for all you have shared with me today. I have been moved to tears several times.

J: THANK YOU GINGER FOR LETTING ME FINALLY EXPRESS HOW MUCH I LOVE YOU AND HOW OLD OUR RELATIONSHIP IS

When Jerry left, I was emotionally elated and drained at the same time. My brain seemed to be bombarded by stimuli that were too rapid to process. My heart felt full of love and admiration for Jerry and his autistic companions. Once again, I wondered who else might be receptive to the content of these recent sessions, when I myself had trouble believing it fully. With extreme caution, I hinted to a few of my closest colleagues about what had been transpiring in the GIM sessions. To my relief, two teachers revealed that they had had similar interchanges with Scott and Twyla, but that they had not felt comfortable speaking to fellow professionals about these instances. We were all afraid of meeting with ridicule and skepticism, especially from colleagues who were denouncing FC.

One teacher, Sarah, recalled that Scott had sensed her meditating during a period of silence. Afterwards, he had amazed her by typing, "I REALLY LIKED YOUR MEDITATION." How did he know what she had been doing in the privacy of her own mind? When I approached Dianne, she disclosed that she had experienced some telepathic exchanges with Jerry. One afternoon at their office, while she was facilitating his typing about a business matter, her mind wandered. In her reverie, she was regretting buying a pair of shoes because she thought they made her legs look fat. Returning to the moment at hand, she checked the computer screen and saw, with astonishment, that Jerry had typed, "DONT WORRY ABOUT THE SHOES YOUR LEGS LOOK FINE." When she accused him of reading her mind, he smiled and typed that he did so regularly. Listening to colleagues' accounts of their unconventional interactions with autistic students eased my anxiety about my own unusual encounters.

I met with Jerry's mother to gauge her reaction to his accounts of his spiritual beliefs. Nora's face was as impassive as her son's usual demeanor while she listened to my report. I was beginning to regret my disclosure when, to my relief, she smiled gently. After a moment's hesitation, she confided that she had had a memorable vision while she was giving birth to his older brother James. In her imagery, she ascended to visit James and another beautiful brown-complexioned baby in a blue one-piece suit. Both babies reached out to her, but she knew that it was right to take only James at that moment. She promised the other baby she would return soon to fetch him. Less than two years later, when Jerry was born, Nora recognized the beautiful little baby from her vision. It did not surprise her that the nurse had dressed him in a blue bunting. Nora told me that she believes that God sends a spirit into each baby, and that babies come into life consciously. She recalled that as a devout Protestant she had read Bible stories to Jerry throughout his childhood. She sensed his interest in spiritual matters, because during these reading periods he had stopped his usual hyperactive movements to sit still and listen attentively. According to Nora, "God is love, and He works directly through autistic ones. Their message of love is crucial as we approach the millennium." During this interview, I recognized that Jerry had a belief system that was compatible with his mother's. Contrary to my fears, she was receptive to hearing about his typed messages about spiritual matters. She asked me to keep her informed about Jerry's revelations.

I felt a renewed determination to be open to whatever Jerry, Scott and Twyla wished to share with me. During her thirty-second GIM session, Twyla and I listened to Mozart's mellifluous *Concerto for Flute and Harp*. She initiated a discussion about dreams:

T: GINGER DO YOU DREAM OF ME?

G: I have had dreams of you, but not recently. Why do you ask?

T: BECAUSE I KNOW THAT JERRY HAS COME INTO YOUR DREAMS

(How did she know that?)

G: I have been trying to tune into him and Scott before I go to sleep so that they can enter my dreams. It is not always successful, but I am interested in learning more about telepathy.

T: I WANT TO HELP TEACH YOU TOO

G: Great. I accept your offer. What do you suggest?

T: I SUGGEST GINGER THAT YOU DREAM OF ME TONIGHT

G: You want to come into my dream tonight?

T: YES SO CLEAR YOUR MIND BEFORE BED. . . . I OFTEN TRY TO VISIT YOU AND YOU DO NOT RECEIVE MY MESSAGES

G: I will try to make my mind more available to receive the messages you are trying to send me. What have you been wanting to communicate?

T: I WANT YOU TO KNOW HOW MUCH I MISS YOU WHEN YOU ARE TRAVELING

G: So especially when I am out of town you try to reach me telepathically?

T: YES AND I FEEL LONELY WHEN I DONT SENSE YOUR PRESENCE

G: Every morning I send you and my other autistic friends a prayer for happiness and good health. Do you ever receive my good wishes for you?

T: YES AND I AM HAPPY THAT YOU TAKE TIME TO SEND THEM

G: I feel good tuning into you each morning. You are teaching me a lot about what is really important in life.

T: LIFE IS SO HARD THAT WARM THOUGHTS HELP A LOT

G: I have been sensing what you would type before you do it.

T: YOU ARE BETTER AT READING MY MIND THAN BEFORE IT MAKES ME HAPPY

G: It makes me happy too, but I wish I could feel more confident about doing that when you and I are apart.

T: GINGER YOU MUST PRACTICE WITH DREAMS

G: Do you enter the dreams of your autistic friends?

T: YES WE ARE ALWAYS VISITING EACH OTHER AT NIGHT

G: So you all are busy at night! Is it easy for you to travel through dreamland?

T: YES BECAUSE I DREAM CONSTANTLY

G: You are always dreaming?

T: YES BUT MUSIC HELPS ME DREAM MORE POSITIVELY

G: That makes sense to me.

T: I WANT TO HEAR THE END OF THIS MOVEMENT WITHOUT YOU TALKING

(We listened in silence for a while. Then Twyla reached for my hand to support her arm as she typed a thought-provoking question.)

T: DO YOU HEAR WHAT I HEAR

G: I think I do, but you may be more sensitive than I am to nuances in the music.

T: GINGER OPEN YOUR EARS AND LISTEN THROUGH MY HEARING

G: You are saying that I can borrow your hearing just as I can read your mind?

T: YES TRY IT AND YOU WILL LOVE THE EXPERIENCE

G. OK. We must stop now, but I'll try it in our next music session.

I reviewed the transcript of Twyla's session before going to bed that night. Intrigued by the idea of listening to music through her synesthetic ears, I remembered that Jerry had suggested earlier on that I adopt his ears to expand my musical receptivity. Although I was not sure how to carry out their advice, I fell asleep feeling grateful for Twyla's efforts to instruct me. The following dream was fresh in my mind the next morning:

*Twyla and her autistic classmate Faith visit me as the embodiment of 'joy'
and 'faith.' The three of us play together happily.*

A few nights later I dreamed a sequel that featured Twyla:

*Mark and I are standing with our luggage at the side of a country road.
We are waiting for an airport limousine to take us to our flight to Mexico.
I see Twyla walking down the road towards me. She is smiling in greeting.
A word is transmitted directly from her mind to mine: "éxquisite." At first
I don't understand because the accent is on the first syllable of the word.
But then the meaning becomes clear: Twyla and I have an exquisite
moment to share before I move away.*

When I reported these dreams about her, Twyla was pleased. She
encouraged me to keep preparing for her to enter my dream life.
Before her final GIM session, I had a dream that centered on her:

*I hear some organ music playing in the attic of an old house and go to
investigate. Someone is giving an impromptu recital on a huge organ.
Twyla is among the members of the audience. As the music enters her
body, she is quivering with delight. I hug her and feel the vibrations entering my own body. We sit right next to each other with our bodies touching
while the music fills us with delightful vibrations. I am aware that other
people notice our intimate connection. I feel proud of my friendship with
Twyla, who is so open and sensitive to the music she loves. She gives me
some sheet music entitled "Good Night."*

Whether or not I would ever actually listen to music with my whole
body, this dream had provided me with a powerful multisensory experience. From Twyla's standpoint, her visiting spirit had entered my dream
to teach me. It was more feasible to me that my own psyche had incorporated aspects of our GIM sessions into exhilarating dream imagery.
But what really mattered was that I was being exposed to different per-
spectives as a result of musical interactions with my autistic students.

CHAPTER NINE

Silent Messages

My dreams were becoming increasingly vivid. They prepared me for startling revelations in Scott's next GIM session:

> S: I WANT TO TALK TO YOU TOO GINGER

(I had not verbalized my desire to reopen our discussion about spiritual matters.)

> S: I HAVE SO MUCH TO TEACH YOU BEFORE YOU TRAVEL THAT I DONT KNOW WHERE TO BEGIN

(I found myself sensing in advance what Scott was about to communicate.)

> G: Well you can begin by knowing that I am getting better at anticipating what you are going to type and at tuning into not only your mind but also the minds of other friends with autism.
> S: YOU ARE A SMART STUDENT BECAUSE YOU HAVE BEEN AROUND FOR MANY LIFETIMES AND I HAVE KNOWN YOU SEVERAL TIMES BEFORE

(Doubts besieged me because I could not recall my birth, let alone a previous existence.)

> G: Can you tell me about another time besides the one in Greece?
> S: YES YOU WERE WITH ME IN WAGNERS DAY WHEN WE WERE PLAYING IN THE SAME ORCHESTRA TOGETHER

(My curiosity overcame my skepticism.)

> G: What instrument did I play?
> S: THE FLUTE
> G: I knew what you would say.
> S: SO WHY DO WE HAVE TO TYPE

(I was unprepared for Scott's assumption that we could rely on telepathy alone.)

G: Because I do not have the confidence that I can read your mind without feeling a connection through typing with you. I will do my best to wean myself from the laptop [computer]. But the other concern I have is that there are a lot of people who doubt the validity of FC and of spiritual realms that they cannot see. I feel a responsibility to keep careful documentation of our conversations so that I can teach other people that autistic souls are wise and have much to teach, despite appearances otherwise. (Scott was just about to attend a national FC conference where he would have a chance to communicate with autistic peers from all over the United States. He knew as well as I did that many professionals in the field of special education still considered FC highly suspect.)

S: YES I GET YOUR CONCERNS AND I THINK YOU ARE WISE TO HAVE SOME SAFEGUARDS

G: But I want you to know that the other night you came to me in my dreams and I felt very open to you being with me.

S: THAT IS GREAT BECAUSE I THINK OF YOU AT NIGHT BEFORE I GO TO SLEEP AND I TRY TO SEND YOU SOME MESSAGES THEN

G: I will make it a practice to stay open to you before I go to sleep and to allow you into my dreams. Do you ever dream about me?

S: YES AND YOU ARE ABLE TO WILL YOURSELF INTO MY DREAMS TOO

G: Do you have any helpful advice on how I can do that?

S: YES JUST THINK OF ME BEFORE BED AND YOUR THOUGHTS WILL REACH ME

G: Really? That is all I need to do? You can receive my thoughts so easily?

S: YES AND SO CAN YOU

G: OK. You are opening up my mind fast! Do you want to play some more music in our final five minutes?

S: YES THANKS FOR LISTENING TO ME

I had difficulty assimilating Scott's assertions. I resisted the idea that one of my young nonverbal students could be instructing me about advanced dreaming techniques. Scott's terminology about willing himself into my dreams reminded me of Carlos Castaneda's accounts of his apprenticeship with Don Juan, a Yaqui Indian seer. In his book *Tales of Power,* Castaneda reported the sorcerer's explanation of the limitations of normal human perception:

"We are perceivers. We are an awareness. We are boundless. The world of objects and solidity is a way of making our passage on earth convenient. It is only a description that was created to help us. We, or rather our 'reason,' forget that the description is only a description. . . . The world that we perceive . . . is an illusion. . . . So, in essence, the world that your reason wants to sustain is the world created by a description and its dogmatic and inviolable rules, which the 'reason' learns to accept and defend. . . . The advantage of the sorcerer is that 'will' is more engulfing than reason" [Castaneda, 1974, pp. 100–101].

Don Juan and other Indian seers presented Castaneda with "unthinkable but real situations" that forced him to realize that his "reason" could cover only a small area of perception. [Castaneda, 1974, p. 248]. Like Castaneda, I was undergoing an apprenticeship with mentors who were demanding that I use my will to extend my awareness beyond ordinary reasoning. Also, like Castaneda, I was wrestling with doubts about accepting instruction from guides who had such an unconventional appearance and spiritual orientation. I reflected on the improbability of a humble carpenter's son claiming that he was the Son of God. Rational people clinging to an ordinary perspective could not accept the miracles of Jesus or his radical teachings about loving the poor and disabled members of society.

These ruminations prepared me for Jerry stretching the boundaries of my consciousness even further in his fifty-fourth GIM session:

G: Would you like me to start the music playing?

J: YES AND DREAM ABOUT ME WHEN YOU TRAVEL

G: I will certainly be tuned into you from Mexico. . . .

J: THIS MUSIC IS FAMILIAR BUT I DONT KNOW WHO COMPOSED IT

G: It is music by a Mexican composer named Manuel Ponce who wrote *Estampas Nocturnas* and the piece that follows, *Cancion Popular.*

J: FRED FEELS VERY DREAMY AND WISHES YOU WOULD TRAVEL WITH FRED IN MEXICO SO FRED CAN SEE WHY YOU LOVE IT SO MUCH

G: How wonderful it would be if you could come visit when I am teaching at La Universidad de las Américas.

J: FRED CAN TRAVEL IN FREDS DREAMS WHEREVER FRED NEEDS TO GO

G: Great. I will expect you to enter my dreams when I am south of the border!

(Jerry turned to look me right in the eyes.)

J: FRED WANTS YOU TO REMEMBER WHAT WE ARE REALLY HERE FOR

(I was jolted into changing the level of our dialogue.)

G: I get it, and I am right here with you for whatever you want to discuss.

J: FRED NEEDS REASSURANCE THAT YOU BELIEVE IN PAST LIVES

(I felt a little defensive.)

G: I believe you, and what you know to be true. I do not recall any past lives myself; but I trust you when you say that we have been together before in another lifetime. Is there more information you want me to have?

J: YES FRED WAS WITH YOU IN WAGNERS DAY TOO WHEN YOU WERE IN THE SAME ORCHESTRA PLAYING THE FLUTE AND FRED PLAYED VIOLIN

(How, I thought, could Jerry be revealing the same information that Scott just reported about a previous lifetime?)

G: You are grinning. I have heard from another person with autism that I played flute in Wagner's orchestra on the opening night of his opera *Parsifal*.

J: THAT WAS SCOTT WHO WAS ANOTHER VIOLIN PLAYER IN OUR ORCHESTRA

G: You are right on! Was anyone else I know there too?

J: FRED REMEMBERS JUST THE PEOPLE WHO FRED IS CLOSE TO NOW LIKE YOU AND SCOTT

G: I feel very connected to Scott and to you. Scott says I was his mother in ancient Greece. Do you know anything about that?

J: YES HE WAS A RELATIVE IN MY PAST BEFORE YOU BECAME MY FATHER

G: Do you and Scott communicate with one another?

J: FRED DOES TELEPATHY WITH SCOTT A LOT AND KNOWS HE WENT TO THE FC CONFERENCE AND LOVED IT

G: I am happy to know that you and he are so connected, because you are both soul mates whom I love deeply.

J: FRED SAYS BE HAPPY THAT WE ARE TOGETHER AGAIN FOR AN IMPORTANT PURPOSE AND WE MUST TEACH PEOPLE ABOUT THE IMPORTANCE OF SEEING BEYOND APPEARANCES TO THE INNER WISDOM AUTISTIC FOLKS HAVE

G: You are laughing and look very pleased.

J: FRED IS SO RELIEVED THAT YOU UNDERSTAND AND ARE WILLING TO HELP ME TEACH MY MESSAGE OF LOVE I AM LAUGHING ABOUT THE COINCIDENCES IN LIFE

G: They are amazing, I agree.

(I shifted to a more mundane topic, because Jerry had been unproductive at work while Dianne was on a two-week vacation to celebrate her wedding.)

G: I hear that you are about to have a change in medication as soon as Dianne returns from her honeymoon. How are you feeling about that?

J: FRED WANTS SOME RELIEF FROM DEPRESSION AND ANXIETY SO MUCH

G: I do not blame you for wanting respite. How are you doing while Dianne is away?

J: FRED FEELS SAD BUT CONNECTED TO HER IN ITALY NOW SHE IS HAPPY WITH MARK AND THAT IS WHAT IS IMPORTANT

G: Is her husband's name Mark or Mike?

J: IT IS MIKE I THINK

G: My husband's name is Mark, you know.

J: FRED KNOWS YOUR HUSBAND FROM BEFORE TOO AND FEELS GOOD THAT YOU ARE TOGETHER

(I felt completely unbalanced by Jerry's declaration.)

G: I appreciate your blessing. Do you want to say more about that?

J: YES MARK WAS IN GREECE TOO AS A CHILD OF YOURS

G: You are laughing again. What is so funny?

J: YOUR SURPRISE ABOUT LEARNING ABOUT PAST LIVES

G: Yes, I feel like a novice in this arena, but I am open to your viewpoint. . . . The music is coming to an end. Do you have anything you want to say before we stop for today?

J: FRED LOVES YOU VERY MUCH AND THANKS YOU FOR LISTENING SO OPENLY

G: I love you very much too.

This session left me in a state of inner turmoil. Although I wanted to believe Jerry, Scott, and Twyla, their shared mythology about living in other eras and asking God to make them autistic messengers of love in this lifetime was so far removed from my own personal belief system that I sensed a powerful cognitive dissonance. I felt dubious about Jerry's allegations of past interconnections with me and Scott. On the other hand, their claims of communicating through telepathy seemed more credible to me. Because the two of them lived in separate residences and had not attended the same school since Jerry graduated years earlier, there was no conventional way that Jerry could have known about Scott attending the FC conference. In my own marriage of many years, my husband and I had noted regular instances of reading each other's mind. As I felt increasingly connected to my autistic students, I could anticipate more frequently what they were going to communicate.

But I had no way of anticipating what Scott would reveal in his next GIM session. I had brought a compact disc of Mexican music to surprise him:

G: This music may be unfamiliar to you, but I think you will like it.
S: I RECOGNIZE IT AS MANUEL PONCE BECAUSE I WAS ALIVE WHEN HE WAS COMPOSING
G: Tell me about that lifetime.
S: I WAS LIVING IN MEXICO AND SO WERE YOU
G: What do you recall about our relationship?
S: WE WERE RELATIVES BUT NOT TOO CLOSE IN THAT LIFE AND I WAS A MUSICIAN WHO KNEW MANUEL PONCE
G: Do you like his music?
S: YES BECAUSE I PLAYED THE VIOLIN AND HE WROTE LOTS OF STRING MUSIC
G: You have had many musical lives.
S: YES THAT IS A THEME IN ALL MY LIFETIMES SAY WHAT YOU WANT TO ASK ME
G: I want to ask you how the FC conference was for you.
S: FREEDOM IS GREAT AND I WAS ABLE TO MEET MANY PEOPLE WITH AUTISM WHO CAN COMMUNICATE WITH ME SO WELL AND FREELY THAT IT MAKES ME HAPPY TO EVEN THINK ABOUT THEM AND I WILL CONTINUE TO COMMUNICATE WITH THEM BY TELEPATHY AND BY WRITING FC LETTERS
G: How is this music affecting you right now?
S: WHEN I HEAR STRING MUSIC I AM UPLIFTED AND HAPPY AND I WISH I COULD STILL PLAY THE VIOLIN
G: Your soul is playing along, and in your imagery you can do it.

S: I WANT TO HEAR MORE STRING MUSIC

G: This next piece starts off with wind instruments but continues with strings. Is that OK.?

S: YES IT IS ALSO BY MANUEL PONCE AND I RECOGNIZE THE PIECE

G: I never knew of his music myself until about a month ago when I found a CD of [Mexican] pieces. Can you explain why you can remember previous lifetimes and I cannot?

S: YOU ARE NOT AS TUNED IN TO YOUR INNER LIFE AS I AM I HAVE SPENT MY WHOLE LIFE IN SILENCE AND FOCUS ON INNER DOMAINS ALL THE TIME

G: I respect how dedicated you are to your inner quest, and I do my best to focus on mine in a very busy verbal world that can be distracting.

S: I KNOW THAT IT IS HARD WHEN YOU TALK TO BE ABLE TO KEEP YOUR MIND STILL ENOUGH TO LISTEN TO WHAT YOU KNOW INSIDE

(Scott was sounding like one of my meditation instructors.)

G: I am anticipating what you are about to type almost every time.

S: THAT IS GREAT YOU ARE LEARNING TO TUNE INTO MY MIND THE WAY I TUNE INTO YOURS. . . . THANK YOU FOR DOING MUSIC WITH ME AND FOR LETTING ME SAY WHAT I NEEDED TO TEACH YOU BECAUSE I LOVE YOU VERY MUCH AND I WILL MISS YOU BADLY.

G: I love you too and do not ever forget that.

S: FRIENDS ARE FOREVER

By the end of this session, I was convinced that I could do a rudimentary form of mind reading. But I was astounded that Scott recognized Manuel Ponce's compositions, which I had just discovered myself. His assertion about yet another past life seemed anticlimactic in comparison. Could that be why I felt so drawn to Mexican people, customs and foods? Because I was just learning Ponce's repertoire, it took me several weeks to validate Scott's statement about the composer's fondness for strings. Although the claims of past lives still seemed farfetched, I wondered how else this autistic boy could have become familiar with such an extensive repertoire of music. Despite my doubts about reincarnation, I trusted the wisdom of my dreams. Because Jerry had requested that I dream of him, I focused on an image of him before going to sleep. The results were gratifying:

I see Jerry shedding his handicaps as if he's taking off clothing. Then he steps into my dream. In the world of dreams, he can move freely and expressively, with none of his usual impediments.

When I told him the content of this dream, Jerry reacted calmly. His typed response was, "THAT IS HOW EVERYONE IS IN DREAMS OUR SOULS HAVE NO HANDICAPS AND MOVE FREELY."

Not long afterwards, I had a memorable dream featuring Scott:

I am not sure if Mark and I are living in the United States or Mexico. Visitors are coming to our home. We are living in a one-story house with a walled-in garden full of flower beds. Scott enters the garden. He is dressed in a three-piece suit and looks grown-up and handsome. As he walks through the garden, the central courtyard is transformed into a labyrinth made of lovely, simple blue and white Mexican tiles. I am amazed by the transformation. Scott starts to read symbols on the tiles as if they are letters of the alphabet—the rudiments of a new language.

The next afternoon I brought a recording of Brahms' piano music for Scott's tenth GIM session:

S: I FEEL GREAT THAT IT IS TIME FOR MUSIC AND I AM EAGER TO HEAR
ABOUT YOUR DREAM LAST NIGHT

(I was stunned by Scott's facility with reading my mind. As I recounted the dream, I sensed that he already knew its contents.)

S: I AM ABLE TO ENTER YOUR DREAMS NOW AND START TO TEACH YOU
THE SYMBOLIC LANGUAGE FOR SPIRITUAL SPEECH. . . .

G: Did you know that you were in my dream last night?

S: YES I COULD FEEL YOU LETTING ME INTO THE GARDEN AND I WAS SO
HAPPY THAT I HAD A CHANCE TO SHOW YOU SOME OF THE SYMBOLS
THAT I USE TO COMMUNICATE WITH MY SPIRIT GUIDES WHO WATCH
OVER ME

(I was not sure what Scott meant by "spirit guides.")

G: Does this music help you access your guides?

S: YES THEY ARE ALWAYS WITH ME AND I KNOW THEY WILL HELP ME
STAY IN TOUCH WITH YOU WHEN YOU MOVE

G: Can you introduce me to your guides? How many are there?

S: THERE ARE TWO ONE GREAT ONE AND ONE LESSER ONE JUST LIKE
YOU HAVE READ ABOUT IN RUDOLF STEINERS BOOK

(Scott had intercepted my thoughts as I was recalling a passage from the Austrian anthroposophist Rudolf Steiner's book *How to Know Higher Worlds*.)

G: How do you know what Steiner taught?

S: BECAUSE I CAN READ YOUR MIND AND I KNOW WHAT YOU ARE
THINKING

G: Can you tell me anything about your guides?

S: THEY KEEP ME ON TRACK AND REMIND ME OF MY HIGHER PURPOSE
IN LIFE AND THEY PROTECT ME FROM DANGERS

G: Do you have a clear image of them?

S: YES I SEE THEM AND I COMMUNICATE WITH THEM REGULARLY THEY
ARE GHOSTLIKE BUT FRIENDLY AND VERY WISE AND CARING ABOUT
YOU AND ME

G: Do you think I have my own spirit guides whom I have not yet met?

S: YES BUT OF COURSE YOU WILL MEET THEM SOON IF YOU KEEP PRAC-
TICING WITH ME BECAUSE YOUR GUIDES KNOW MINE

(Scott must have sensed my incredulity, because he ran to the bathroom. We ended the session soon afterwards.)

I resisted the concept of ghostly mentors wafting around us. Although I had read accounts of such phenomena, I had trouble believing that spirit guides were watching over us as we were conversing. Equally mystifying to me was how an autistic adolescent could comprehend Rudolph Steiner's twentieth century religious system that grew out of theosophy and centered on human development [Steiner, 1994]. While I was in the midst of these musings, Jerry gave me one of his poems—which was strikingly relevant:

> *Soul Friends*
> We return to a life
> Without a clear understanding
> Of that which awaits us.
> We know that we must learn and grow

And seek the truths
Of our very existence.
Quiet contemplation reveals secrets
Burning in our souls.
Every aspect of our lives yearns to teach.
Deep connection with our spiritual guides
Show us the way to friends
Who share a path of love, truth and light.
Where is the life I expected to see?
Where is the knowledge I expected to acquire?
Seek the truth; hold it close to your heart
And share it with that special soul mate.
Then the light of understanding will shine.
Forever mine, soul friend.

Jerry's poem referred to spiritual guides who seemed to give him the same kind of support that Scott claimed his own guides provided. Like Scott, Jerry was tuning in to my current interest in Rudolph Steiner's writings about spirit guides. Because Scott could read my mind so fluently, I wondered if my thoughts were purely my own or if my reflections might be emerging from a shared pool that Carl Jung called the "collective unconscious." I was reminded of the philosopher David Abram's description of the world view of Navajo Native Americans:

For the Navajo, then, the Air—particularly in its capacity to provide awareness, thought, and speech—has properties that European, alphabetic civilization has traditionally ascribed to an interior, individual "mind" or "psyche." Yet by attributing these powers to the Air, and by insisting that the "Winds within us" are thoroughly continuous with the Wind at large—with the invisible medium in which we are immersed—the Navajo elders suggest that that which we call "mind" is not ours, is not a human possession. Rather, mind as Wind is a property of the encompassing world, in which humans—like all other beings—participate. One's individual awareness, the sense of a relatively personal self or psyche, is simply that part of the enveloping Air that circulates within, through, and around one's particular body . . . [David Abram, 1996, p. 237].

It was through my dreams that I could relate most easily to the Navajo belief in an all-encompassing mind. I could dream about my autistic friends and understand their viewpoints free from doubts and the censorship of rational thoughts. Although I felt highly motivated to keep communicating with Jerry, Scott, and Twyla through dreams, the stress of preparing to move to Mexico interfered with my dream life. In the fall of 1996, I had trouble sleeping deeply during the night, and I seldom recalled more than fragmentary images the following morning. Excerpts from Jerry's fifty-ninth GIM session show his concern with my state of mind:

G: What kind of music would you like to listen to now?
J: FRED WOULD LIKE BACH SONATAS WITH STRINGS

(I played a recording of Bach's first three sonatas for cello and piano.)

G: How does this music make you feel?
J: FRED LOVES THE ORDER AND CLARITY IN BACHS MUSIC
G: I understand completely because right now I feel the calming effects of such structured harmonies and such clean melodic lines.
J: DO YOU THINK OF ME AT NIGHT BEFORE BED

(I felt like a child being reprimanded for forgotten homework.)

G: Yes, I do, as I promised, but lately I have been busy traveling, and I have been going to bed very late and feeling tired.
J: FRED WORRIES THAT YOU ARE NOT TUNING IN ENOUGH TO LEARN WHAT I NEED TO TEACH YOU BEFORE YOU MOVE
G: I will do my best to slow down and to get to bed at a reasonable hour, so that my concentration will be better before I go to sleep. I want to learn whatever you wish to teach me. Is there anything you want to tell me now?
J: FRED KNOWS YOU ARE UNDER A LOT OF STRESS WITH WORRIES ABOUT MOVING BUT IT IS IMPORTANT FOR YOUR SOUL TO HEAR FROM FREDS WISDOM
G: I know that what you say is true. I have been anticipating each phrase before you type it so I am on your wavelength much more easily than I used to be.
J: FRED SENSES YOU READING FREDS MIND AND IT MAKES FRED HAPPY BECAUSE FRED NEEDS REASSURANCE THAT YOU ARE GROWING SPIRITUALLY
G: How do I make the transition from reading your mind while touching your hand to doing it without typing together?
J: FRED READS YOUR MIND REGULARLY WHENEVER FRED SEES YOU

(I had a sudden flashback to an incident during the previous support group meeting.)

G: Did you know what I was thinking when I looked over at you during the Beethoven piece in the FC support group?

J: YES I KNEW YOU WERE SENDING ME LOVE AND I RETURNED LOVE TO YOU DID YOU FEEL IT

G: I sensed it but then doubted my ability to receive your nonverbal message from across the room.

J: FRED SAYS DO NOT DOUBT GINGER BECAUSE FRED SENDS YOU MESSAGES A LOT AND WANTS YOU TO RECEIVE THEM WITHOUT CENSORING THEM

G: I will practice trusting my perceptions more. You have already given me confidence in my mind-reading capacity.

J: FRED SEES YOUR TIREDNESS AND WANTS YOU TO REST BETTER

(I was touched that Jerry cared about my well-being. His capacity for empathy did not fit the classic profile of autism.)

G: Any recommendations on how to slow down?

J: FRED SAYS BREATHE DEEPLY AND STOP TRYING TO GET SO MUCH DONE EVERY DAY

G: Good advice! How are you feeling with your medications now?

J: FRED FEELS BETTER AND LESS COMPULSIVE AND SPACY THAN BEFORE

G: I sensed that you were having an easier time lately and I'm glad it's true.

J: FRED SEES YOUR ARM HURTS WHILE FACILITATING AND FRED DOES NOT WANT TO ADD TO THE PAIN

(Jerry had noticed that I was wearing a brace on my wrist.)

G: Thanks for your concern, but communicating with you is so important to me that a little arm strain is well worth it. How is this faster music for you?

J: FRED LISTENS TO THE DREAM MUSIC AND FEELS SAFE AND CONTAINED IN THE NOTES AS THEY MAKE FREDS BODY FEEL CALM AND FREE AND GINGER YOU ARE NOT READING MY MIND RIGHT NOW NOW YOU ARE PAYING ATTENTION AGAIN I NEED TO FEEL IN HARMONY WITH YOU AND NOT SENSE YOUR DISTRACTIONS

G: You caught me red-handed thinking about other things in the middle of your message. Your powers of concentration are hard to match, but I will shape up!

J: FRED SENSES YOU TUNING IN NOW AND FRED WANTS YOU TO LET IN THE MUSIC BECAUSE IT WILL HELP YOU FEEL LESS TIRED AND ANXIOUS SO YOU CAN RELAX AND ENJOY SUCH BEAUTIFUL SOUNDS YOU ARE SHARING FREDS MUSICAL MIND AND LEARNING THE LANGUAGE OF MUSICAL ENERGY

(I wondered which of us was the real music therapist.)

G: I have always been drawn to music but I have not taken such refuge in it as you have, and sometimes I forget to appreciate it as much as it deserves. The sacred quality of music is so precious, and you remind me of that.

J: FRED SEES YOU CRYING AND FRED FEELS GOOD THAT YOU KNOW HOW SACRED MUSIC IS IT SPEAKS DIRECTLY TO YOUR SOUL

G: What is your earliest memory of music?

J: FRED REMEMBERS HEARING WAGNERS MUSIC WHEN FRED LIVED IN ANOTHER LIFETIME BUT IN THIS LIFETIME FRED SAYS MUSIC WAS THERE FROM INSIDE THE WOMB WITH SOUNDS FROM MY MOTHERS BODY AND FROM OUTSIDE HER

G: So right from the start of consciousness you were aware of musical rhythms and sounds. Your memory is extraordinary.

J: FRED REMEMBERS EVERYTHING THAT EVER HAPPENED IN DREAMS AND IN AWAKE LIFE

G: Wow! I am truly impressed, because I feel as if my own memory is sketchy. The music has just come to an end, and it is about time for us to stop for today, but do you have any last words of wisdom?

J: GINGER THANK YOU FOR PLAYING SUCH BEAUTIFUL MUSIC AND FOR TUNING INTO MY MIND SO WELL

After this session, I reviewed a number of music therapy studies regarding prenatal auditory responses. S. Peiper [Peiper, 1925] discovered that the five-week-old fetus reacts with sudden movements to loud sounds that originate outside the mother's body. During a project at the Eastman School of Music, Donald Shetler found that some fetuses of five months could discriminate between two musical selections that had contrasting tempos. While stereo earphones played directly on their mothers' abdomens, ten fetuses responded with sharp agitated movements to stimulating music and with rolling or more muted movements to slower, sedative music [Shetler, 1989]. I had no difficulty accepting that a fetus could have prenatal musical experiences, but I wondered how, in his late twenties, Jerry could recollect such occurrences. Despite recalling Dr. Cytowic's finding that many synesthetes have especially strong memories, I doubted an adult's capacity to remember fetal music appreciation sessions. In the final weeks of music therapy sessions with my autistic friends, my mind was full of unresolved questions.

Chapter Ten

Farewells

I usually looked forward to holiday time at the year's end, but in November 1996 my students and I were suffering through a painful termination process. For us, New Year's Day meant the start of my new life in Mexico. Before my departure, I asked Twyla, Jerry, and Scott for permission to write about their musical journeys. Their mothers had already given me their consent, but I wanted to be absolutely sure that I had the blessing of my autistic students. All three granted me permission without any reservations. Part of Scott's response follows:

S: I WANT TO STAY IN TOUCH WITH YOU BECAUSE YOU WILL WRITE MY STORY AND I WANT TO KEEP YOU INFORMED ABOUT THE INNER WORLD OF PEOPLE WITH AUTISM

G: I feel very humble and honored that you think I am worthy of such trust.

S: I AM SURE THAT YOU ARE MY MOTHER AND MY SOULMATE SO THERE IS NO DOUBT IN MY MIND THAT YOU ARE THE RIGHT PERSON TO WRITE ABOUT ME AND MY GOALS AND WHY I AM REALLY HERE

Jerry responded to my proposal in an equally affirming manner:

J: FRED FEELS GOOD THAT YOU WANT TO WRITE ABOUT FREDS SPIRITUAL BELIEFS BECAUSE FRED WANTS PEOPLE TO UNDERSTAND WHY AUTISTIC PEOPLE HAVE COME HERE TO TEACH ABOUT THE POWER OF LOVE AND THAT APPEARANCES ARE NOT THE ESSENCE OF OUR SOULS

G: You have a great deal to teach people, and I would be honored to write about your mission, if you think it would help get the word out.

J: FRED KNOWS THAT YOU WILL WRITE WITH INTEGRITY AND FRED TRUSTS YOU TO TELL WHAT IS SAFE TO TELL

G: Do you have any fears that some people might not understand?

J: FRED IS USED TO PEOPLE NOT UNDERSTANDING AND FRED BELIEVES IT IS TIME FOR PEOPLE TO WAKE UP TO THE NONMATERIAL WORLD AROUND THEM

Twyla gave me a positive response in her own pragmatic style:

T: I WANT YOU TO WRITE ABOUT ME

G: I thank you for your confidence in me. . . .

T: HAVE YOU ASKED ANYONE ELSE

G: Yes, I have spoken to Jerry and Scott about this writing project.

T: DO THEY AGREE

G: They have agreed to let me tell their stories because they think
the stories will give hope to other people with autism.

T: I THINK SO TOO AND I WANT TO BE PART OF THE PROJECT

Twyla expressed alarm that she would be graduating from school the
following spring. She had realistic fears that she might be placed in a
group home or a work setting where nobody would facilitate her typing.
She wrung her hands and twisted clumps of her hair in between bursts of
typing about how anxious she felt about the possibility of losing all the
gains of the previous months. I resonated with her dread that "AUTISM
WILL TAKE OVER AGAIN." She wanted me to help her fight against being
sentenced once again to a state of isolated silence. I promised to advocate
for Twyla's right to type. Soon afterwards, I met with her Planning and
Placement Team. I was relieved that her mother and the teachers and
administrators who had witnessed Twyla's recent progress all joined me in
supporting her continued access to FC. Despite doubts about whether
local, state or federal funds would be used to hire an experienced facilitator, the consensus was that this young woman with autism deserved the
right to self-expression and that FC provided that avenue.

As we met for our final GIM session, Twyla was contending with
separation anxiety on many levels. I was touched that she was able to
focus on my impending departure:

T: I AM SAD ABOUT YOU MOVING AWAY

G: I feel sad too, but I want to treasure the time we have together.
I brought some beautiful music for you to listen to today.

T: THANK YOU GINGER I WANT TO DREAM TO MUSIC

G: See if you recognize the piece.

T: IT IS BACH I THINK

G: It is a motet by Palestrina who was a composer in the sixteenth
century.

T: DREAMS COME WITH THIS MUSIC

G: Do you have dream images?

T: YES I SEE YOU AND ME IN MEXICO TOGETHER

G: What are we doing in Mexico?

T: WE ARE WALKING OUTSIDE AND PLAYING TOGETHER
G: What is your mood?
T: I FEEL GOOD BEING WITH YOU AND I WANT TO TRAVEL
G: You seem ready to travel.

(Twyla sneezed twice loudly.)

T: I SNEEZE WHEN I FEEL GOOD
G: Why are sneezes connected to feeling good?
T: BECAUSE I CAN RELEASE SAD FEELINGS
G: I like the idea of sneezing away sad feelings.
T: I HAVE MANY WAYS TO HELP MYSELF FEEL BETTER
G: What are some other ways that you help yourself? It is so important to have inner resources that help you through times of change in your life.
T: I HELP MYSELF BY DREAMING WITH FRIENDS LIKE YOU AND JERRY AND YOU MUST PRACTICE MORE
G: You are right. I have been so stressed about moving that I have not been paying attention to my dreams. I too must take care of myself during so much change.
T: YOU FEEL TIRED TO ME AND DEPRESSED
G: You are right; but, like you, I have ways to help myself feel better.
T: THAT IS GOOD BECAUSE I WANT YOU TO FEEL HAPPY
G: I sense you wanting me to feel happy, as you do all your friends. You have a loving heart.
T: YOU DO TOO GINGER AND I WANT YOU TO REST MORE
G: I will rest more because without rest we all lose our sense of humor. [That's] what often helps most during times of upheaval.
T: SENSE OF HUMOR IS MY GIFT IN THIS WORLD OF AUTISM
G: You have a particular gift of seeing the humor in what could be a tragic situation.
T: WHEN I THINK IT CANT GET WORSE IT DOES SO I TRY TO BE CALM
G: What helps you most to be calm?
T: I SING TO MYSELF AND I LISTEN TO MUSIC LIKE NOW
G: Do you like this ancient vocal music?
T: YES IT IS SLOW AND CALM AND SOOTHING
G: This kind of music soothes me too because it is steady and predictable in its harmonies. It makes me feel good that this music has been around for hundreds of years calming listeners from all over the world.

T: YES MUSIC CAN GO ACROSS CULTURES SO YOU AND I CAN ENJOY THE
SAME PIECES OF MUSIC WHEREVER YOU GO

G: That is an important realization that no matter what country I
visit, music will serve as a link between us.

T: I FEEL BETTER THINKING OF THE MUSIC AS A CHAIN OF SOUND
BETWEEN US

G: I like your words. You have a poetic way of writing.

T: I AM A POET AT HEART LIKE JERRY AND MICHAEL [a member of the
FC support group].

G: Jerry and Michael and you can offer the nonautistic world
many insights about your experiences, and your poetic writing
can teach people to be more tolerant of those with differences.

T: GINGER I SAY GO FOR IT AND LET YOUR DREAMS LEAD YOU

G: Thanks for the tip. I will try to do as you say.

T: THE DREAM ROAD CAN BE SO WONDROUS

G: I know how wondrous dreams can be, and I have received
much support from my dreams.

T: I DO TOO SO WE HAVE THAT IN COMMON

G: I already knew that you and I have a lot in common. You are a
kindred soul.

T: THANKS GINGER I AM YOUR FRIEND FOR LIFE

G: It feels great to have a friend for life!

T: THANK YOU FOR LISTENING TO MUSIC WITH ME AND LISTENING TO
MY ADVICE.

G: I listen to you because you give good advice.

Twyla tolerated a brief farewell hug. As she walked purposefully
away from me toward her classroom, I watched her stocky body and
unruly golden hair. I had utmost respect for her courage and determination to surmount the challenges of autism. My affection for this poet
who took friendship so seriously was strong and indelible.

Scott's final GIM session was a wrenching experience for both of
us. When he entered the music room in a noisy burst of wild activity, I
was afraid that our energy levels were too polarized for us to cope
with our grief:

G: You seem to be in a great mood right now, humming and leaping and bouncing.

S: I FEEL SILLY BECAUSE I DO NOT WANT TO FEEL SAD THAT YOU ARE
LEAVING

G: I know that sometimes silliness can cover up sad feelings . . . I think we need to deal with the real feelings.

S: I WANT TO LISTEN TO MUSIC NOW

G: You have been beating the Vibratone [a percussive instrument] hard and fast. How did that feel?

S: IT FELT LIKE A RELEASE OF TENSION BECAUSE I FEEL SO TIGHT AND WORRIED ABOUT YOU GOING AWAY

G: It is good that you found a musical way to release your tension. I am starting a recording of some soothing music, and I will scratch your back.

S: THIS MUSIC IS CALMING AND I FEEL LESS SILLY

G: You look much calmer now. This is Celtic music from Ireland and Wales.

(I was playing excerpts from a compact disc entitled *Celtic Legacy*.)

G: It comes from far away and from across centuries of time. This music puts our separation into perspective because music can connect us through time and space.

S: I WANT TO STAY CONNECTED WITH YOU ALL MY LIFE

G: I feel the same way. I will write and visit and stay in touch. How does the harp music make you feel?

S: THE HARP IS SO LIQUID AND FLOWING AND IT WASHES AWAY MY WORRIES

G: Let the harp give you comfort.

S: I FEEL BETTER JUST BEING HERE LISTENING TO MUSIC WITH YOU IT IS SO NICE NOT TO HAVE TO DO ANYTHING BUT TO RECEIVE MUSIC AND FEEL HEALING ENERGY

G: It is a gentle moment to treasure in our lives.

S: I WANT TO COME INTO YOUR DREAMS AGAIN TO TEACH YOU ABOUT HOW TO TRAVEL THROUGH TIME AND SPACE WITH ME WILL YOU LET ME INTO YOUR DREAM TONIGHT

G: I will be as open as possible to you before I go to sleep. Then I must trust that you know how to enter my dreams.

S: I COME OFTEN AND SO MANY TIMES YOU ARE CLOSED IN WORRIES OR TIGHT LITTLE DREAMS I CANT FIT INTO BUT IF YOU KEEP OPENING UP YOUR MIND THERE WILL BE SPACE FOR ME

G: Thanks for the instructions. Do you have any imagery with this chanting?

S: THE CHANTING IS REALLY NICE AND IT SOOTHES ME CALMING ME DOWN AND HELPING ME BE PATIENT

G: Patience is such a difficult virtue to develop. The music has ended for today's session. Would you like to sing the "Goodbye Waltz" with me?

S: YES AND VISIT ME IN YOUR DREAMS

I was in tears as I waved good-bye to the blond young man with the unbalanced face and the awkward gait. Although I tried to see Scott objectively, I knew what a rare soul lay inside his ungainly body. I felt that an invisible bond would connect us, no matter how far apart we might be physically.

My most challenging separation process was with Jerry, whose eight years of music therapy had benefited us both profoundly. His sixty-first GIM session involved our attempts to find positive aspects of a transition that was as difficult for me as it was for him:

J: THIS IS FAURES REQUIEM AND I LOVE IT BECAUSE IT IS SO PRO-FOUND AND SPIRITUAL

G: As we face finding a replacement for me doing music with you, I thought we could both use some spiritual nurturing.

J: DREAMING TO THIS PIECE MAKES ME FEEL BOTH SAD AND HOPEFUL BECAUSE IT IS ABOUT DEATH AND RESURRECTION

G: Can you relate to the theme of dying and being reborn?

J: YES I FEEL LIKE YOUR MOVING AWAY IS A DEATH OF OUR RELATION-SHIP IN THIS FORM BUT THAT WE WILL BE FRIENDS IN A WHOLE NEW REBORN WAY

G: I agree with you that our friendship will evolve in dimensions that we may not expect now. A mix of sadness and affirmation is embodied in this music.

J: DREAMING TO MUSIC BRINGS PEACE TO MY SOUL AND HELPS ME CALM DOWN ABOUT LIFES CHANGES

G: Sometimes music feels like it is the only stable yet mobile force in life. This piece will sustain me in Mexico as it does here. . . .

J: DREAMING ABOUT FLYING TO MEXICO IS A NEW THEME FOR ME AND I ENJOY REHEARSING FLYING TO VISIT YOU

G: The idea of meeting your flight in Mexico City makes me feel happy.

J: FRED DREAMS OF GOING THERE A LOT BECAUSE MEXICO IS A SPIR-ITUAL HOME FOR YOU AND I WANT TO SEE WHY YOU LOVE IT SO MUCH

G: You spend so much of your time focusing on spiritual domains. I believe that you would like the rituals and religious ceremonies that are so prevalent in Mexico. Many Mexicans have a deep faith in God to see them through difficult economic and political times.

For Jerry's last GIM session, I played a recording of Beethoven's *Symphony No. 7*. I sensed that we both needed forceful and expansive music to support us during our mourning process:

G: You spend much of your time focused on the immaterial world. Is music like this a bridge to that realm?

J: YES BEETHOVEN SPENT MUCH OF HIS TIME IN SPIRITUAL REALMS AND HIS MUSIC IS DIVINELY INSPIRED SO I FEEL THAT INSPIRES ENERGY IN MY BODY AND IMAGES ABOUT GODS PLAN FOR US ON EARTH

G: What can you say about God's plan for us on earth?

J: FRED SENSES THAT GOD KNOWS WHO IS DESERVING OF HIS LOVE AND GOD WILL REMEMBER THOSE WHO LOVE AUTISTIC PEOPLE AND GOD KNOWS THE GOALS OF AUTISTIC PEOPLE ARE TO DELIVER GODS MESSAGE OF LOVE TO THOSE WHO PAY ATTENTION

G: So underlying your daily obstacles and hardships you have a faith that your life has a crucial purpose. You have touched many people with your loving heart, and you have woken them up to the talents and profound thoughts that lie beneath your autistic surface.

J: FRED FEELS YOU STRUGGLING TO STAY PRESENT WHEN YOU HAVE SO MUCH ON YOUR MIND AND WHEN YOU ARE TIRED BUT STAY PRESENT BECAUSE THIS MUSIC IS ABOUT THE TRIUMPH OF THE WILL DURING ADVERSE TIMES THIS SEVENTH SYMPHONY IS VERY DIFFERENT FROM THE FIFTH BECAUSE THE SEVENTH HAS A GENTLE QUALITY THAT PERSUADES LISTENERS THAT THEY CAN TRUST IN GOD EVEN WHEN THEY HAVE DOUBTS

G: This music can serve as a connector between us when we live far apart. Whenever I hear the seventh symphony, I will think of your words and let the music reaffirm my trust in the universe.

J: FRED KNOWS HOW MUCH YOU LOVE FRED AND DOES NOT DOUBT YOUR PRESENCE FRED IS SAD ABOUT TIME RUNNING OUT IN THIS SESSION ...

G: Let us treasure this time together. This third movement has so much joy in it. We can breathe in some of the joy of loving each other as good friends.

J: FRED LOVES YOU AND LISTENING TO BEETHOVENS MUSIC WITH YOU
BECAUSE YOU FEEL THE JOY IN HIS MUSIC AND RELATE TO FREDS
WORLD OF MUSIC

Jerry towered over me as he let me hug him good-bye. His gentle brown eyes peered down at me through his new eyeglasses. I could hardly see through my tears as Dianne arrived to drive him to his group home. He was not alone in being unable to speak. I felt enormously grateful for the lessons in patience and perseverance and love that this tall quiet man had taught me. But my feelings were beyond words. What was clear to me was that my soul's path was inextricably woven together with Jerry's.

Epilogue

Before they departed, Dianne coached Jerry to give me a farewell gift from both of them. It was one of his poems that she had matted and framed. This poem now hangs in my office at La Universidad de las Américas in Cholula, Mexico. It reminds me of my friends with autism and the musical journeys we shared:

> *Souls Dancing*
> Years ago I pleaded guilty
> To the crime of disability.
> What a terrifying reality
> This admission brought to my world.
> Sadness and fear
> Were all I knew
> For many years.
> There seemed to be no escape
> From the efforts involved
> With just getting by.
> Then came this beautiful soul
> Who floated into my life
> On a cloud of soft music.
> She taught me to reach within,
> To touch the forgiving
> And loving teacher and friend,
> Where just knowledge
> Of a deep and spiritual nature
> Could thrive.

Companions who travel together are inevitably changed as much by one another as they are by their journey. Scott and Twyla conveyed in their own ways what Jerry's farewell poem expresses: gratitude for my tapping their musical and spiritual depths. Thanks to the three of them, I have had to examine some of my basic beliefs and to open up my heart and mind. A year after our separation, I can see more clearly how their devotion to inner growth matches my own.

Since childhood, I have kept a personal journal. At the age of ten, when my mother gave me my first diary, I was aware that an interior life of reflection accompanied my exterior life of activity. In adolescence I began my daily practice of writing down and analyzing my dreams. Although I am not certain where my interest in spirituality originated, I have felt compelled to understand the workings of my mind and to examine my purpose in life. My spiritual life has expanded outside the traditional religious framework of my Episcopalian background. In my daily meditation practice, I concentrate on my breath rising and falling, noting when I am distracted by thoughts or by physical sensations, and returning to my breath. I am convinced that sitting quietly to clear my mind for a half hour each day helps me maintain my balance in our complex and rapidly moving world.

I feel lucky to be married to a man who shares my belief in the value of inner exploration. On our extensive travels, I have met people with a similar involvement in spiritual practices despite differences in backgrounds, customs, and languages. Mark and I are both drawn to the spiritual traditions of past cultures. We have gazed at Greek temples in the Mediterranean, explored cathedrals all over Europe, climbed Mayan pyramids in the jungles of Mexico and Guatemala, watched the sun rise over Inca temples at Machu Picchu in Peru, and witnessed the ancient stone statues on Easter Island under the light of a full moon. When contemplating the architectural and artistic remains of past civilizations, I feel reassured by the evidence that human beings have consistently devoted time and energy to honoring the sacred in the midst of their daily tasks.

On a journey to Dharamsala, India, Mark and I took daily walks to a monastery where Tibetan monks living in exile chant their early morning prayers. A high point of our trip was having an audience with His Holiness the Dalai Lama, whose wisdom, compassion, and joyful presence profoundly affected us. I was struck by how beautifully the Dalai Lama practices what he preaches. Not only does he speak about the need to develop a 'good heart' and to embrace enemies as teachers, but he also spreads compassionate wisdom in all of his daily encounters. As Jerry, Scott, and Twyla revealed their 'good hearts' to me, I sensed the proximity of their message of love to the Dalai Lama's teachings.

I recognize how eclectic my spiritual questing has become. I do not think that any one religion or culture has all the answers for achieving inner happiness and fulfillment. As our world evolves into a global community, I benefit from being open to a variety of mentors and spiritual traditions, using what works in my own life. Jerry, Scott, and Twyla have taught me to look beyond surface appearances and to respect a belief system that helps them make sense out of being born with autism. Recalling how many hours they spend in silent reflection and in conscious dreaming motivates me to maintain my own disciplines, meditating, and noting my dreams. Whenever I start to feel sorry for myself in the face of life's adversities, I remember how hard it is for my three autistic friends to control their awkward bodies, to communicate in a verbal world, and to reconcile their sensory perceptions with those of normal people. I celebrate their ability to transcend daunting disabilities and to devote themselves to teaching those who will pay attention to treat all beings with loving respect.

If they were given the opportunity, consider how many other silent souls might echo Jerry's courageous statement: "I WANT TO SEE HOW MY MIND WORKS WITH THE MUSIC."

Bibliography

Abram, D. (1996). *The spell of the sensuous: Perception and language in a more-than-human world.* New York: Pantheon Books.

Biklen, D. (1993). *Communication unbound: How facilitated communication is challenging traditional views of autism and ability/disability.* New York: Columbia University, Teachers College Press.

Bonny, H. (1978). *The role of taped music programs in the GIM process.* Monograph No. 2. Salina, KS: Bonny Foundation.

Bruinicks, R., et al. (1996). *Inventory for client and agency planning (ICAP).* New York: Riverside Publishing.

Castaneda, C. (1974). *Tales of power.* New York: Simon and Schuster.

Celtic Legacy (1995). [selections from various groups including W. Coulter, Orion, The Barra McNeils, et al.] Narada Collection Series (Compact Disc ND-63916). Omaha, NE: Narada Music.

Clark, M. F., and Keiser, L. H. (1989). *Teaching guided imagery and music: An experiential-didactic approach.* Garrett Park, MD: Archedigm Publications.

Clarkson, G. (1991). "Music therapy for a nonverbal autistic adult." In Bruscia, K. (Ed.), *Case studies in music therapy* (pp. 373–385). Phoenixville, PA: Barcelona Publishers.

Cytowic, R. (1993). *The man who tasted shapes.* New York: G.P. Putnam's Sons.

Darling, D. (1993). *Eight string religion.* Compact disc HS 11037-2. San Francisco, CA: Hearts of Space.

Donnellan, A. & Leary, M. (1995). *Movement differences and diversity in autism/mental retardation: Appreciating and accommodating people with communication and behavior challenges.* Madison, WI: DRI Press.

Eliasoph, E. & Donnellan, A. (1995). "A group therapy program for individuals indentified as autistic who are without speech and use facilitated communication." In *International Journal of Group Psychotherapy,* 43 (3), pp. 549–560.

Galway, J. (1994). *The lark in the clear air.* Compact disc 9026-61379-2. New York: BMG Music, Inc.

James, W. (1901/1990). *The varieties of religious experience.* New York: Vantage Books.

Jenkins, K. *Adiemus* (1995). Compact disc 7524-2. London: Virgin Records Ltd., Jenkins Ratledge Ltd. USA distribution: Caroline Records, Inc.

Kellogg, J. (1984). *Mandala: Path of beauty.* Lightfoot, VA: MARI.

Kugelmass, I.N. (1970). *The autistic child.* Springfield, IL: Charles C. Thomas.

Leiter Test, available through the McGuire Media Center. Kurksville, MO: Trumann State University.

Martin, R. (1994/1995). *Out of silence.* New York: Penguin Books, by arrangement with Henry Holt and Company.

Mayer-Johnson, R. (1992). *The picture communication symbols.* Solana Beach, CA: Mayer-Johnson Company.

Musica Mexicana (1990) [a collection featuring the works of Mexican composers including Chavez, C., Ponce, M., and Revueltas, S. performed primarily by the Mexico City Philharmonic/Enrique Batiz.] Compact disc DCA 738. London: Academy Sound and Vision, Ltd.

Nordoff, P. & Robbins, C. (1983). *Music therapy in special education,* second revised edition. St. Louis, MO: MMB Music, Inc.

Peiper, S. (1925). Cerebral function in infancy and childhood, (B. Nagler & H. Nagler, Translators) In Wortis, J. (Ed.), *International Behavioral Sciences Series.* New York: Consultants Bureau. See also Wilson, F. & Roehmann, F. (1990). *Music and child development.* St. Louis, MO: MMB Music, Inc.

Rocha, A. & Jorde, K. (1995). *A child of eternity: An extraordinary young girl's message from the world beyond.* [with a foreword by J. Borysenko.] New York: Ballantine Books.

Shetler, D. (1989, Spring). "The inquiry into prenatal musical experience: A report of the eastman project 1980–1987." *Pre- and Perinatal Psychology Journal,* 3 (3), pp. 185–189.

Steiner, R. (1994). *How to know higher worlds.* Hudson, NY: Anthroposophic Press.

Williams, D. (1992). *Nobody nowhere.* New York: Avon Books.

Williams, D. (1994). *Somebody somewhere.* New York: Random House.